Journal
OF THE
Royal Asiatic
Society
China

Vol. 83   2023   No. 1

PUBLISHED EXCLUSIVELY FOR MEMBERS OF THE SOCIETY

The Journal of the Royal Asiatic Society China is published by
Earnshaw Books on behalf of the Royal Asiatic Society China

Journal

OF THE

Royal Asiatic Society China

Vol. 83 No. 1, 2023

EDITOR
Melinda Liu

Copyright 2023 RAS China

—◇◦◇—

CONTRIBUTIONS
The editor of the Journal invites submission of original unpublished
scholarly articles, essays and reviews on the religion and philosophy,
art and architecture, archaeology, anthropology,
environment and current affairs
of China and Greater Asia. Books sent for review will be donated to the Royal
Asiatic Society China Library. Contributors will receive copies of the Journal.

LIBRARY POLICY
Copies and back issues of the Journal are available at the Royal Asiatic
Society China Library. The library is available to members.

https://ras-china.org/

—◄▬▬►—

Journal of the Royal Asiatic Society China
Vol. 83 No. 1, 2023

978-988-8843-50-3

EB 209

Front Cover Image: Canadian anthropolgist and educator Isabel Crook (left),
who witnessed more than a century of China's tumultous history, died in 2023
at the age of 107. Photo: Wikipedia. Colourisation: Hava

Designed and produced for RAS China by Earnshaw Books Ltd
17/F, Siu Ying Commercial Building, 151-155 Queen's Road Central, Hong Kong

*The Royal Asiatic Society China thanks Earnshaw Books
for its valuable contribution and support.*

DISCLAIMER

The opinions expressed in this publication are those of the authors. They do not purport to reflect the opinions or views of the Royal Asiatic Society China or its members. The designations employed in this publication and the presentation of material therein do not imply the expression of any opinion whatsoever on the part of RAS China.

CONTENTS

SECTION 3: LIVES WELL LIVED

SECTION 4: REVIEWS AND PASSAGES

LETTER FROM THE EDITOR

Anniversaries often trigger reflections, and this year the Journal of the Royal Asiatic Society China experienced plenty of both. 2023 marked the 165th year since the journal was first published in June 1858—also the year when the North China Branch of the Royal Asiatic Society (NCBRAS) was launched. Later, reflecting how global perceptions of Chinese power centers shifted northward, the erstwhile NCBRAS became today's Royal Asiatic Society China in Shanghai.

Meanwhile in 2023 the Royal Asiatic Society—the London-based "mother ship" of the global RAS community—celebrated its Bicentenary with a series of impressive publications, exhibitions, and events, including an unforgettable commemorative journey to Rajasthan, in which I was honoured to participate. In Beijing, the Royal Asiatic Society Beijing (RASBJ) celebrated its 10th birthday; more anniversary news appears in Rachel Rapaport's RAS China Annual Report.

Just before this journal went to print, China marked the first anniversary of the end of the government's stringent "zero COVID" policies. From early 2020 to December 2022, pandemic-era government restrictions limited travel and in-person gatherings. A newfound sense of liberation in 2023—after nearly three years of quarantines, mass testing and lockdowns—inevitably triggered a frenzy of tourism, dining out, and partying—as well as a deep sense of reflection and questioning. What happened during that dark period? What sort of "new" normal should we be experiencing now? Has life changed for good?

COVID-19 showed that our worlds shrink and expand, depending on lived experience. Even though memories of lockdowns and pandemic restrictions have receded, some of us remain acutely aware of how friends morphed into small faces on small screens, how life shrank into a tiny world—and how a tempest in a teacup could take on disproportionate importance, at least for a time.

The first section of the RAS China Journal examines this phenomenon: China's worlds within worlds. Award-winning writer Paul French describes a comparatively minor incident which ruffled the delicate plumage of foreign diplomats who roosted in the elite Peking Club in 1896. Author Margaret Sun shares a compelling narrative about wartime adversity, starting over, grief, and ultimate contentment, told through the vehicle of an apartment building at 156 Peking Road, her former Shanghai home. Pierre-Henri Biger's article also opens gradually—focused on the history, structure and uses of Chinese fans—then accelerates to address dramatic, big-picture events.

A second section, 'Annals and Archives', reflects on diverse aspects of the RAS legacy. Former RAS China Journal editor Fiona Lindsay Shen guides us through the archives in California of Florence Ayscough, born in Shanghai in 1875, who served as librarian for the NCBRAS.

Dr. Elizabeth Driver presents a rich, memorable account of the RAS Bicentenary tour of Rajasthan, which followed in the footsteps of Col James Tod in 1819-1822 when he was the first political agent for the East India Company. Tod became a founding RAS member and the Society's first Librarian.

A central piece in this year's journal is by Peter Hibbard, who in 2007 became the first President of the Royal Asiatic Society China in Shanghai. His story is an evocative and valuable record of the revival of the society and its library in mainland China after NCBRAS had ceased activities in 1952.

Don't miss author Mark O'Neill's piece on Zhou Youguang, the father of China's Pinyin system, whose far-reaching achievements and resilient character were extraordinary. Other stories of resilience, equally enthralling, come from diverse archives. Rare family documents and hitherto unpublished photographs allowed contributors Christine Maiwald and Paul Sofronoff to evoke the dramatic China experiences of older relatives—who, respectively, were a German merchant-diplomat in wartime China and a Siberian-born celebrity racehorse trainer of Old Shanghai and Hong Kong.

The Journal's final section, 'Reviews and Passages' offers an array of book reviews, as well as tributes to people who've passed away. Sinologist Frances Wood conveys her delight in perusing *The Peking Express*, a hot first book by Beijing lawyer James Zimmerman. Paul French explores how one could learn about China at a time when no one knew much about China, in his review of *Chinese Dreams: in Romantic England: the Life and Times of Thomas Manning* written by Edward Weech, the current librarian of the London RAS Library. Writer Jen Lin-Liu introduces *Autobiography of a Chinese Woman* by

Buwei Yang Chao who wrote a 1947 cookbook and has been dubbed "the Julia Child of China". RAS China Council Member Katherine Song assesses the life and work of Chinese film director Chen Jianlin, who died in 2022.

One of the saddest moments this year, for those of us who knew her, was the August 2023 death of educator and anthropologist Isabel Crook, born in Chengdu to Canadian missionary parents in 1915.

Many thanks to editors Tracey Willard, Kate Munro, Warren Singh Bartlett and others who went to great lengths to help produce this year's journal. Special gratitude goes to Journal advisors Robert Martin and James Miller for their wise counsel, as well as to the team at Earnshaw Books and to publisher Graham Earnshaw for his enthusiasm and support.

We would love to hear your feedback—and your suggestions for future contributions to the RAS China Journal. Have you been working on a rollicking tale about China or Asia? Stumbled across a hidden archive of dusty documents deserving wider attention? Feel free to email your comments and proposals to raschina@ras-china.org

Melinda Liu
Editor

RAS CHINA COUNCIL 2022-2023

Honorary President
Christopher Wood–British Consul General Shanghai

Honorary Vice Presidents
Carma Elliott CMG, OBE
Peter Hibbard MBE
Liu Wei
Tess Johnston

Vice President
Rachel Rapaport

Treasurer
Jenny Yang

Membership Director
Vittorio Blasi

Secretary
Marta Lopez

Journal Editor
Melinda Liu

Librarian
Sven Serrano

Convenors
Julie Chun (Art Focus)
Katherine Song (Film Club)
Robert Martin (Stories of Things)
James Miller (Philosophy Club)
Jonathan Crowder (Non-Fiction Book Club)

NON-COUNCIL POSITIONS

Administration Manager
Irina Carpenco

Fiction Book Club
Dagmar Borchard

Library Volunteers
Kyle Bisman, Julie Chun, Liang Ping,
Diane Long, Robert Martin, Coquina Restrepo,
Compton Tothill, Zhang Dasheng, Summer Xia

RAS CHINA ANNUAL REPORT 2022-2023

The past year has been one of recovery and transition. Shortly after our Annual General Meeting last year, the country opened up to the world, ending nearly three years of pandemic control. Worries about being stuck inside turned into worries about getting sick. By the Spring Festival, things had largely returned to "normal," or a variant of it. We were able to gather in May for a social event to mark the bicentenary of the Royal Asiatic Society's founding and the belated 15th anniversary of RAS China's re-establishment in Shanghai.

Event Highlights: Our programming recovered this year, with 46 events plus a collection of online lectures shared by our partner branches in Beijing, Hong Kong and Korea. We held several online and hybrid events as well, allowing our overseas members to connect virtually and giving us the ability to function despite sporadic Covid outbreaks.

General Programmes had a tasteful line-up of programming this year, with several food & beverage events including a deep-dive into Chinese noodle-making and culture, and gin, coffee, wine and plum wine tastings. We enjoyed book talks about the Uchiyama Bookstore, the British scholar of Chinese Thomas Manning, and growing up in 90s rural China. We also had two guided museum tours, one at the Urban Planning Museum and one at the Jiushi Art Museum for an exhibit on the famous architect Tong Jun.

The Art Focus group continued with the theme of Places & Spaces, this year with a focus on Art in a Global Context. Participants took part in active discussions at several museums including the Rockbund Art Museum, the newly opened contemporary-focused START Museum, the Shanghai Center of Photography, and the relocated Yuz Museum in the resuscitated ancient town of Panlong. We were also able to explore two in-depth studies, including a comprehensive overview of the art museum landscape in Shanghai and a fascinating research of early 20th century cigarette advertisements by convener Julie Chun. In addition, we were introduced to the little-known Buddhist iconography of hooded monks by the young scholar Jinchao Zhao; and a unique lecture about photography and advertising by the Curator Rebecca Morse in collaboration with the Los Angeles County Museum of Art.

2023 also marks the 10-year anniversary of Art Focus. Since the group's inception in 2013, Julie has convened a total of 96 events, and delivered approximately 60 lectures on a wide variety of topics on classical and contemporary art in China to consistently provide high-quality, and engaging content to our Society. We are extremely thankful to Julie for a decade of service, and to the countless museums, artists and curators who gave their time freely for Art Focus.

The Film Club took advantage of the return to normalcy with five in-person film screenings: *Mao's Last Dancer*, the inspirational true story of a ballet dancer who went from rural China to the world stage; Zhang Yimou's highly acclaimed, award-winning *Raise the Red Lantern*; *Mountains May Depart*, a Jia Zhangke masterpiece about social shifts under China's relent pursuit of economic development; Japanese war film *Merry Christmas, Mr. Lawrence*, featuring scores by the prominent musician Sakamoto Ryuichi who also starred in the film; and *In the Heat of the Sun*, Jiang Wen's coming-of-age tale about freewheeling teenage boys in 1970s Beijing. We also organized a special group visit to the 25th Shanghai International Film Festival in June to watch Xie Jin's epic *The Opium War*.

Stories of Things brought us items as small as a hairy monkey figurine, as large as a resurrected 1930s bookstore, and everything in between, including a silver urn, a collection of paper crafts used as offerings for the deceased, Cultural Revolution paper cuttings, century-old embroidery and a wooden couplet. We also had an exclusive indie rock music performance.

The Asian Philosophies and Religions group took us deep into the world of mysticism. The season started with a comprehensive overview of mysticism in the East and West with convener James Miller. Yitzhak Lewis delved into the Jewish mystical philosophy of Kabbalah, Ben Van Overmeire explored the sudden versus gradual enlightenment debate of Zen Buddhism, and Bogna Konior connected erotic mysticism written by various female Christian mystics in earlier centuries to the cyberfeminism of today. Each lecture concluded with time for socialisation and a dinner for participants to carry on the philosophical conversations.

The Non-fiction Book Club returned to an in-person format after a long period of online discussions. We looked back at the turbulence of the early 20th century with Emily Hahn's *China to Me*, Graham Peck's *Two Kinds of Time*, and Tim Harper's *Underground Asia*. Xiaowei

Wang's *Blockchain Chicken Farm* and Megan Walsh's *The Subplot* analysed fast-changing contemporary China. And Thomas Mullaney's *The Chinese Typewriter* connected old and new.

The Fiction Book club also returned after a lengthy absence. We started the season with Wang Anyi's *Fu Ping* and Tan Twang Eng's *The Garden of Evening Mists*, before returning in November with Tash Aw's *We, the Survivors*.

Library and Reading Room: Last September, we moved our substantial collection of books and DVDs from our library space at the House of Roosevelt to the RAS Reading Room near the West Bund, which had previously housed a portion of our collection. Thanks to the tireless work of our Head Librarian Sven Serrano and dedicated library volunteers, we were able to pack, transport, unpack and reshelve our books just in time to re-launch the space as a main library for our AGM. We also have sent 18 boxes of books about art and architecture on permanent loan to the Urban Archeo library that is opening in the building adjacent to the original headquarters of RAS China. Once the library opens later this year, those books will be available for a wide range of people to enjoy.

We now hold regular library hours at the Reading Room four days a week and have welcomed scholars from near and afar to view our collection. We have also held eight events in the Reading Room or adjoining café, and we look forward to regularly hosting our two book clubs there. We are immensely grateful to Steven Lin at HWCD for providing this beautiful space for our collection and activities.

RAS China Journal: The 2023 Journal features topics ranging from Paul French's peek at an obscure diplomatic fracas within the 1896 Peking Club to Frances Wood's review of the new book "Peking Express". Several authors also reflected on the RAS legacy, to mark this year's anniversaries celebrated by the global RAS community.

Membership: RAS membership is recovering more slowly from the pandemic's expatriate exodus than we would have liked. Membership and donor signups started to pick up in the fall as a new batch of foreigners arrived in Shanghai, but we are still significantly lower than in pre-Covid times. As we have not raised our membership dues since our re-establishment in 2007, we hope that our current members as well as prospective new members can appreciate the value we provide to the community at a relatively low cost. We are committed to increasing our presence as a stand-out cultural organization and strengthening our membership ranks in the coming year.

Finances: RAS China's finances began to recover this year after last year's hit due to the pandemic-control protocols. Our cash reserve is around RMB 200,000. Revenue from membership and PRC donations exceeded that of last year but is still significantly lower than in 2021. For our programming overall, we were just above break-even when accounting for event costs. Besides this year's Spring Social, our major standard expenses this year were the Glue-up fee (our online membership and event management platform), the administrative manager's salary and the AGM.

Rachel Rapaport
Vice President RAS China

RAS China Memberships and Donations 2022-2023
Honorary Memberships

Honorary Members	7
Fellows of RAS China	2
Complimentary Institutional memberships	4

Paid Memberships
Membership Type

- Individual Members	70
- Joint/Family Members	32
- Student Members	0
- Young Professional Members	6
- Overseas—Individual Members	6
- Overseas—Household	0
- Lifetime Members	4
GRAND TOTAL	127

RAS Donor Friends

- Individual Donors	20
- Joint/Family Donors	3
- Young Professional Donors	9
- Student Donors	0
- Institutional Donors	1
GRAND TOTAL	33

RAS China Events, 27 Nov 2022—25 Nov 2023

- General Program (Rachel Rapaport)	10
- Art Focus (Julie Chun)	8
- Film Club (Katherine Song)	6
- Non-Fiction Book Club (Jonathan Crowder)	6
- Fiction Book Club (Dagmar Borchard)	3
- Stories of Things (Robert Martin)	5
- Asian Philosophies and Religions (James Miller)	4
- Shared events with RAS Beijing	1
- Additional RASBJ online lectures shared with members	8
- Additional RASHK online lectures shared with members	4
- Additional RAS Korea online lectures shared with members	5
- Special Events (Journal Launch, Spring Social and AGM)	3
TOTAL	63

SECTION 1

China in Microcosm

TROUBLE AT THE PEKING CLUB IN 1896
By Paul French

ABSTRACT

In 1896 all seemed relatively calm in the Peking Legation Quarter. However, among the foreign diplomatic corps in the city, issues of protocol, hierarchies and resentments simmered just below the surface. That year they were to boil over and cause strife and argument in the Legation Quarter's most venerable institution, the Peking Club.

THE PEKING GOLDFISH BOWL

It was a storm in a teacup, a minor squabble that should really have been of no consequence. But this argument took place in the close-knit Legation Quarter of Peking where the diplomats of a couple of dozen countries lived cheek-by-jowl and saw each other almost daily. In the late summer of 1896 the combination of the intense seasonal heat, the annual dust storms, and the vagaries of Peking diplomatic conventions combined to create the greatest scandal the venerable Peking Club had ever seen. Ensconced within the Legation Quarter, the Peking diplomats—who often referred to themselves as 'dipsis'— had a major falling out. Naturally the issue they all got upset about was protocol.

In the late nineteenth and early twentieth century it was commonplace to describe the extreme incestuousness of Legation Quarter society. The French diplomat Alexis Leger, also well-regarded as a poet by the pen name Saint-John Perse, noted that 'The Peking diplomatic corps has created within the confines of the Legation Quarter its own very special, cocoon-like mode of life'.[1] Slightly later, W. Somerset Maugham, visiting and attending a Legation Quarter diplomatic dinner party, recalled that, 'They were bored to death with one another.'[2] A few years after Maugham, Peter Fleming, the travel writing older brother of James Bond creator Ian, described the denizens of the Legation Quarter as living in a goldfish bowl, 'fish in an aquarium going round and round … serene and glassy-eyed'.[3] Occasionally there would be flashes of excitement, terror even. The Boxer Uprising and the Siege of the Legations in 1900. Tricky questions

Figure 1: The Peking Club

such as what to do with the old Tsarists that occupied the Russian Legation after the 1917 Russian Revolution ousted them and the communists announced they wanted to take control of the embassy. Or scandals that shook the moral compasses of the Quarter—such as in 1921 when the wife of the Italian ambassador tried to murder the fiancee of her naval captain lover in the Grand Hôtel des Wagon-lits and had to be bundled out of the country after her paramour shot himself in the Italian Legation's grounds.[4]

But in 1896, Boxers, Bolsheviks and dipsis with murderous intent were still to come. All was relatively calm in Peking. The world wars, revolutions and scandals that would set diplomat against diplomat remained ahead. But trouble reared its head anyway in the dark wood-panelled dining rooms and carpeted reading rooms of the most status-conscious establishment of the status-conscious Legation Quarter—the Peking Club. When Great War flying ace and aeroplane salesman in China Cecil Lewis described the Legation Quarter in the 1920s as mired in 'ridiculous petty protocol', he perhaps never realised that thus was it ever.[5]

THE RATTLE RATTLES

What might have remained an argument within the stuffy confines of the Peking Club went international thanks to a gossipy periodical in Shanghai. The China Coast publishers Kelly & Walsh had launched

The Rattle in early 1896, an illustrated periodical loosely based on the English publication *Punch* (or *The London Charivari*).[A]

Such publications, mixing humour, gossip, doggerel, caricatures and cartoons, had been tried before on the China Coast—*Puck*, also known as *The Shanghai Charivari*, a Shanghai-based illustrated humour magazine from a quarter century earlier.[B] *The Rattle's* slogan was aimed at the easily amused, those 'pleased with a rattle, tickled with a straw', a line from Alexander Pope's 1734 *Essay on Man*. Ultimately the mix didn't work too well in China and *The Rattle* failed to emulate the success of *Punch* in Britain. The magazine folded barely a year later in 1897, relaunched briefly in 1900, but soon folded again. However, it was in print in August 1896 and published the following piece of anonymous doggerel which appeared to be mocking all those involved in a spat at the exclusive Peking Club.

Elegy on the Peking Club
(With apologies to Oliver Goldsmith)[6]

Good people all of every sort
Come, listen to my song:
If it be short, the more you ought
To ponder on it long.

In far Peking, since many a year,
There doth exist a Club
For exiled foreigners, a queer
Ramshackle sort of tub.

'Tis there Peking Diplomacy
Doth from its labours rest
(Though where and what those labours be
Diplomacy knows best).

Here everyday at eventide
Or earlier, for some,

A   *Punch* was founded in 1841 by Henry Mayhew and wood-engraver Ebenezer Landells. The publication effectively coined the term 'cartoon' and was a great success.
B   A charivari being a European and North American folk custom designed to shame a member of the community, by way of a parade accompanied by a discordant mock serenade.

They let the fate of nations slide
And take their *otium cum*.[C]

Now till quite recently, they say,
'Twas good to see the Powers
All friendly, at the close of day
Beguile the fleeting hours.

Then all was cheerful Harmony,
Each Minister, so kind,
Would feed the hungry frequently
(As often as he dined).

But to Peking a Minister
There came, all recently,
From sunny France; a Minister
Plenipotentiaree.

(Of Ministers, as none dispute,
Full many kinds there be,
But this was one of high repute,
Quite Extraordinaree.)

The Club and he at first were friends
Until—now here's the rub—
H.E., to gain some private ends,[D]
Got mad, and left the Club;

Resigned—and so (for this affair
Was High Diplomacy)
Did *Chanceliers* and *Secretaires*
And clerks of low degree.

And next, because their love for France—
Blind love—had made them blind,
The Russians straightaway joined the dance
And one and all resigned.

C   leisure with dignity
D   His Excellency

Then everywhere, as all might see,
We gossip and hubbub,
And many blamed Diplomacy
That marred so good a Club:

While others said, with visage sad,
And accents muttered low,
That "things were looking pretty bad,
The Club was bound to go."

But soon a wonder came to mock
This view and prove it wrong,
The Club recovered from the shock
And now is going strong.[7]

THE PEKING CLUB

What on earth had occurred?

The Peking Club was one of a number of clubs in the Legation Quarter. Many of them came and went—old boys clubs for alumni of British public schools, retired Imperial Customs staff, the French Club for those of that nationality or preference, clubs for those with military associations or common interests, such as the Danish Book Club (for employees of the Great Northern Telegraph Company) or the Thatched House Club for members of Britain's Geological Society.[E] Many of these clubs actually met in the Peking Club, the grand old man of Legation Quarter Clubs.

The Peking Club, occasionally referred to as either the Pekin Club, or Peking Country Club in some memoirs, had been established in the early 1890s initially just behind the German Legation on Wall Street, so-called as it ran directly alongside the Tartar Wall, the southern boundary of the Legation Quarter, before later moving to improved and larger premises situated between Rue Marco Polo (now Taijichang Dajie), Rue du Club and Rue Hart (both now subsumed) behind the French Legation and Barracks. The Club initially had between forty and fifty members, a number that quickly grew, and included a reading room, billiards room, card tables, and a tennis court. Major attractions were the apparently quite decent lunch, the well-stocked bar, the range

---

E   Which had itself been formed in 1824 at the Thatched House Tavern in St. James's Street, London.

of imported foreign newspapers available and, later, a Reuters telegram news feed. The building was what was then called Comprador-style; a hybrid architectural style found along the China Coast, Hong Kong and Southeast Asia with verandas and arched windows.

Membership was primarily the corps of European dipsis, some business and military men and various other notable members of the city's 'Foreign Colony'. It was male only. It was not to everyone's taste. Reginald Johnston, British diplomat, Former Commissioner of Weihaiwei (Weihai), and later tutor to last emperor Puyi, thought most members completely ignorant of political matters in China.[8]

Un Grand Scandale

On 21 March 1896, news of the row in Peking emerged in the international newspapers, probably derived from local stringers in Peking or *The Rattle*. The *Glasgow Herald* in Scotland reported, 'Hitherto the Ministers of the different European countries and their leading nationals have met harmoniously at the Peking Club. That, however, is now changed and the French members, followed of course by the Russians, have all resigned'. [9]

The cause of the arguments was one of the Legation Quarter's best-known foreigners, the Russian Ambassador Count Cassini. The Count—his full name and title being Arturo Paul Nicholas Cassini, Marquis de Capuzzuchi de Bologna, Count de Cassini—was a lifelong Russian diplomat. His family were Russian, of Italian lineage. He was born in 1863, graduated from the Foreign Office Academy in St Petersburg in 1854 and served in various European postings until being sent to Peking in 1891.

Cassini had been the Russian diplomat to announce Tsarist imperial ambitions in Asia—the completion of the Trans-Siberian Railway as well as extracting the long-term concession of Port Arthur (Lushun). Cassini is said to have said that 'To possess the East, Russia must possess the Liaotung (Liaodong) peninsula'.

However, it had been announced that Cassini was moving postings that

Figure 2: Count Cassini in 1903

October—to eventually become Russian Ambassador to the United States. Still he was due to remain in post in Peking for another six months at least. And that's where, remembering Cecil Lewis's quote that the Legation Quarter was mired in 'ridiculous petty protocol', the trouble started.

At the annual Club elections the Count was not appointed to the board, as were automatically the British *chargé* and the American and German ministers. This despite the fact that the German minister, Gustav Freiherr Schenck zu Schweinsberg, was also due to soon depart Peking. At this apparent slight—all ministers were normally automatically appointed to the board—the French members of the Club resigned *en masse*. The French persuaded the Russian members that their ambassador had been insulted and so they too resigned.

SECRET TREATIES

British nationals formed the majority of the club's members and felt that they had not slighted Count Cassini as he was about to depart Peking. It is not clear if they were aware of Schenck zu Schweinsberg's imminent departure too. A fly was thrown into the ointment in that, after Cassini had announced his intention to leave for his new posting, he actually remained some months longer, refusing to leave until the Chinese had signed the one-sided so-called Li–Lobanov Treaty, also known as the Sino-Russian Treaty of Alliance, between Russian Foreign Minister Aleksey Lobanov-Rostovsky and Viceroy Li Hongzhang. The treaty largely dealt with granting Russia additional railway concessions in north-east China and the creation of the China Eastern Railway. The Li–Lobanov Treaty was seen as unfair by the Chinese and even the *Chicago Tribune* reported in December when the details became public that the agreement was, in practise, the creation of a 'Russian protectorate' in Manchuria.[10] In London *The Times* considered that Cassini had quietly outmanoeuvred all the other European powers in China through increasing Russian influence considerably in the north-east.[11]

However, it was not apparently widely known outside Russian circles in Peking that Cassini would remain until everything regarding the treaty and the China Eastern Railway was finally concluded to St Petersburg's satisfaction. And so his departure was delayed by over a year. Count Cassini finally took over the Washington embassy from the departing Russian ambassador Otto von Kotzebue in late 1898.

With Cassini gone to America the scandal seems to have blown over. Despite French outrage the Russians had never seemed that worried about the protocol misstep anyway. Cassini and St Petersburg were playing a larger game in north-east China that successfully cemented Russia's position in Manchuria for two decades until the Russian Revolution swept them and their treaties away. In Shanghai *The Rattle* got some fun out of it all, but fairly quickly the gossip quietened down in the Peking Club reading room, the diners got on with their lunches, the billiards players their games and the Peking Club slunk back into the general state of torpor that was its normal condition… at least for a couple of years until the Boxer Uprising shattered the peace and quiet of the Legation Quarter once again.

Paul French *is the author of* Midnight in Peking, *a New York Times Bestseller, and* City of Devils: A Shanghai Noir. *His next book* Her Lotus Year: The Mysterious China Sojourn of the Woman Who Became the Duchess of Windsor *will be published in 2024.*

REFERENCES

1. Saint-John Perse (Alexis Leger), *Letters*, Princeton University Press, 1979, p.258.
2. W. Somerset Maugham, 'Dinner Parties: The Legation Quarter', *On a Chinese Screen* (London: Heinemann, 1922).
3. Peter Fleming, *News From Tartary*, (London: Jonathan Cape, 1936).
4. See, Paul French, 'An Affair to Remember', *South China Morning Post Weekend Magazine*, August 27, 2022, pp.14-17.
5. Cecil Lewis, *All My Yesterdays*, (London: Element Books, 1993), p.35.
6. Citing *An Elegy on the Death of a Mad Dog* (1766), actually a satire of an elegy by the Irish poet and playwright Oliver Goldsmith (1728-74) about a rabid dog that bites a man, and the effect that this act of violence has on the people of London. It is in reality a comic satire on the way outward appearances are often at odds with private feelings and behaviours.
7. Anonymous, *The Rattle*, August 1896, (Shanghai: Kelly & Walsh). The spelling and italics are reproduced as in the periodical.
8. Reginald F Johnston, *Twilight in the Forbidden City*, (London: Victor Gollancz, 1934), p.380.
9. 'Social and Personal', *Glasgow Herald*, March 21, 1896, p.7.

10. 'Treaty of Russia and China', *Chicago Tribune*, December 13, 1896, p.11.
11. 'The Manchuria Railway', *The Times* (London), January 1, 1897, p.12.

THE CHINA TRUST COMPANY BUILDING, SHANGHAI: LIFE AT 156 PEKING ROAD

By Margaret Sun

ABSTRACT

Margaret Sun was born in Shanghai in 1935 into a Cantonese family of modest means. During the dying days of Shanghai's Concessions era, she grew up speaking (and even thinking) in English except when she was at home, thanks to her family's contacts with the city's Eurasian community through the church they attended. Like many Cantonese in Shanghai at the time, Sun's father made his living as a Chinese 'dragoman', a link between the Shanghainese and the city's foreign businesses. Having a foot in both worlds, he belonged to neither. His family lived a precarious existence. As the Communist army approached and later, as the new government was established, the Suns became the subject of scrutiny. Young Margaret's existence was heavily defined by the multicultural, multigenerational building she and her family lived in on the corner of Peking and Sichuan Road—The China Trust Building, later known as the Peking Apartments. Almost seven decades after she left Shanghai for good, she can still recall names, dates and (often pithy) details. Her slice of life reminiscences reveal a side of 1930s and 1940s Shanghai often eclipsed in grander narratives.

THE NEIGHBORHOOD

The China Trust Company (中国信托公司) is situated on the curb of Peking Road and Sichuan Road, facing to the south and the west. It was probably built in the late 1800s, or the very beginning of the 1900s, when Shanghai was undergoing a new surge in its quest to become an even more modern city. The location was ideal in that it was only two very short blocks to the waterfront and the Bund, and the building stood on a square block that faced Hong Kong Road to the north, Peking Road to the south, Sichuan Road to the west, and Museum Road (today's Huqiu Road) to the east. The four-story building housed offices for the different departmental heads of each of the CTC's business sections on the second floor, which could be accessed via the entrance on 156 Peking Road, or via a backdoor and up the back stairs from the alleyway behind. The offices were right on the corner, with entrances to the left and right that led to a curved counter with desks behind it, much like any other bank. The building's exterior has remained untouched over the years, even though the exterior of the building across the road was cleaned up for the state visit of Queen Elizabeth II in 1986.

The owners of the CTC building were Cantonese. They departed for the US right after the Japanese invasion began in the early 1930s, and left the management of their business to a Shanghainese by the name of Mr. Gu, a scheming and chinless meany.

Mr. Gu lost no time in downsizing the company, vacating all the rooms on the second floor so that he could rent them out as soon as the rightful owners were out of the country, to the flood of refugees flowing into the International Settlement from the other side of Soochow Creek.

Immediately upon entry to 156, which had polished terrazzo floors, two and half flights of stairs lined with metal balustrades and topped by nice, shiny wooden bannisters, gave access to the rest of the building. The first half flight led to a small room just large enough for a bed for the night watchman. Then next two flights led to a hallway with painted wooden floors, where odd numbered rooms were on the right and even numbered rooms were on the left. Rooms 2,4 and 6 faced Peking Road, while Rooms 10, 12, 14, 16 and 17 faced Sichuan Road. These rooms all had small balconies, but measured just under 12 square meters in size. Only Rooms 16 and 17 were larger.

The odd numbered rooms faced the backyard, and some did not even have windows, as they were originally intended as storage places for brooms, mops, buckets, and other necessities used by the caretakers to keep the building clean. All the rooms with balconies had through passages. They were connected to each other by a door in the left wall, and their hallway entrance doors bore the name of the department they had once housed, as well as the name of the former head of that department, on marbled glass.

At the end of the hallway was a single toilet which consisted of two commodes in separate cubicles and a urinal. Close to this was a washbasin, and a big square concrete basin with a single tap the caretakers used to wash their brooms and mops. A continuing flight of stairs led from the second floor to a square terrazzo landing, and then another flight of stairs led to the third floor, which was a large empty space at the time.

It had been a kind of recreational area, where the staff had eaten lunch. Nearly all the big companies provided lunch for their staff in those days, and caterers would come each day at noon with big bamboo steamers, one or two layers deep, carried on bamboo shoulder poles, that contained rice and many small dishes that changed every day. It also had billiard tables, card tables, and ping pong tables. At the end of the third-floor hall was a toilet, which was right above the one on the floor below. A final flight of stairs led to the fourth floor, which consisted of single and double occupancy rooms meant for the use of unmarried staff members. Any spare rooms were originally rented out to college students. Their toilet was also right above the toilet on the floor below.

All the even numbered rooms with balconies had a radiator, and heat had originally been supplied by a big furnace in a boiler room in the backyard. We moved in on August 13, 1937, when the Japanese threatened to cut the traffic from Hongkew to the British Settlement. Mr. Gu dismantled all the radiators, as heat hadn't been supplied since the rightful owners had left, and the residents couldn't afford heating anyway. We were glad to have the radiators removed, as space was precious. He had also wanted to remove all the pipes along the hallway ceiling to sell the metal for scrap, but the project proved too big to be worth his while.

Figure 1: The former China Trust Company building in Shanghai

To get an idea of the block where the CTC was located, coming out of 156 Peking Road and turning left led to what had been the China Sunday School Union and the China Christian Bookstore on the corner of Peking Road and Museum Road. Their building was also four storeys tall. It was followed by several shops that sold laces, embroidered items, and other expensive goods. All, without exception, were owned by Swatownese (people from Shantou in Guangdong). The largest was the Oriental Star, which was near the end of the block.

Facing this block, from the corner of Peking Road and Museum Road was a tall building called the China Industrial Bank (中国实业银行), which had a long flight of marble stairs leading up to its business section. Then came the former museum, which was also a very solid building, and then a slightly less well-built building just before arriving at the striking Beth Aharon Synagogue. Then came a cluster of other buildings, both residential and commercial, some of which were foreign owned. The synagogue was turned into a factory during the Cultural Revolution, and then razed in 1985.

Back to the long line of Swatownese lace shops, there was another building, which ended on the corner of Museum Road and Hong Kong Road, that housed the Banker's Club. Across from that was the China Bible House. Further along the block were a few shops, and then on the corner of Hong Kong and Sichuan roads, there was the Navy YMCA Building, which took up the entire corner.

The Ward Building was right next door. This apartment building, four or five storeys tall, was home to a few foreign families, including the Hansens. The head of the Hansen household, a blue-eyed Dane who worked for ICI, lived with his wife, whom I knew as Auntie Mabel (née Johnston), and their son Ivor. There was also the Sylvestri family, a couple with two children, and a bachelor by the name of Louis Bojeson, who was half-Chinese and half-Danish, who happened to have been my father's schoolmate at Saint Francis Xavier College, and an old lady we all called Samyi Ahpaw (三姨阿婆), or Grandma Samyi. She lived with her daughter Elizabeth Ward, whom we knew as Auntie Ellie. She and Auntie Mabel were cousins, their mothers were sisters, and members of the Ford family, who were also Eurasians.

Our Neighbours
The Ward Building was owned by Thomas Ward, another Eurasian, and Elizabeth Ward's father. I was told that he came from humble

beginnings, starting out as an office boy at the Shanghai Municipal Council. One of his duties was to fill the teacups of foreigners during meetings to discuss the future of the city. Thomas spoke Cantonese, Shanghainese and some English, and was clever enough to understand a little of what he overheard and saw. During these meetings, parts of the city identified for development were circled on large maps. Thomas would visit those areas and inform the shop-owners and families there to up their property prices if foreigners offered to buy them out. In exchange, he told them that if his advice turned out to be helpful, they could give him a little something in return. Naturally, being privy to the discussions at the municipality, things usually worked out the way he said.

In time, Thomas felt that he ought to be the one to benefit from his knowledge, and he began to buy properties in areas slated for redevelopment under an assumed name, using loans from a money lender. When the municipality people came to buy the entire street, he would make a pile, and became richer by the day, as much construction was taking place. To make a long story short, he became very rich, and I was told that he had once chartered a ship to take all of his relatives to Tsingtao for a summer holiday. He also sent Alice Ford, the youngest sister of his first wife, Samyi Ahpaw, to France to be educated. When she returned, they married.

Thomas and Alice had two children, Stephen and Valery, who were sent to England early on because their father's reputation was getting out of hand. Thomas eventually lost both of his legs to syphilis, as there were no effective drugs those days, but even a double amputation did not keep him from getting richer. They lived on the top floor of a building that had once housed the well-known newspaper 文汇报 (Wen Hui Bao) across from the back gate of the British Consulate on Yuanmingyuan Road, which is now a pedestrian street. Thomas' first marriage to Samyi Ahpaw was Chinese, complete with a sedan chair and whatnot, but it was not registered at the British Consulate. However, his marriage to Alice was, as was his eldest daughter. He even registered two daughters he had with his mistress under his name.

Next to the Ward Building was a very large and very expensive furniture shop called 毛全泰 (Mao Quan Tai). It had tall show windows on either side of its entrance, which opened onto a flight of stairs set against an elaborately painted background. In one of the show windows there was always an elegant dining-room set, complete with dining-table, chandelier, sideboard, buffet and other expensive items. The other show window usually displayed an equally expensive bedroom set-up, with a big double-bed, boudoir, wardrobe, chest-of-drawers, and all the other trimmings. 毛全泰 would change the contents of their show windows about twice a year. The workshop that made the expensive pieces displayed in them was just behind the store.

Adjacent to the furniture shop there were one or two small shops, a pharmacy, a tailor and a tobacconist. Behind them all was Tengfeng Li (腾风里), or Flying Phoenix Lane, where the furniture workshop was located and which led to an ordinary Chinese residential area of one and two-storey residences. The back entrances to the stores on Sichuan Road were all here, too. Tengfeng Li led to the back door of the CTC and to 156 Peking Street and was home to a very large warehouse, which we used to call a 'godown', which was guarded by a Sikh policeman. Then came a dry cleaner's, which had its (literal) 'sweat' shop on the lane. The dry cleaner's was also a laundry, and the only one in the area, so it was always extremely busy, because it had a monopoly on all the business from Sassoon House, the Palace Hotel, the Cathay Hotel as well as of all the foreign residents of the Embankment Building and other buildings in the area.

Next came a shop that sold cigarettes, and then a cobbler shop run by a Cantonese mother-and-son team, which was next to a tailor shop making men's suits, run by a Ningbo man whose family lived in the loft behind the store, and who slept on the shop floor at night. Above these two shops were the balconies of Rooms 14, 16, and 17 of the China Trust Building. This now brings us back to the Sichuan Road side of the corner on which our building stood.

The Shanghai Trust Company (上海信托公司) was on the corresponding corner. The STC was a better building than the CTC, although like the CTC, its exterior remained unchanged in the years that followed. It was only a four or five-storey building, but it had an elevator. On the Peking Road side next to the STC was the Zhejiang Bank, another building much better built than either the STC or the CTC, and across from it was an apartment building. The Zimmermann family lived there. The father must have had a British passport, because he was interned during the war, but the mother and the three daughters, Marjorie, Lily, and Rita, were not. Marjorie was around my age.

Figure 2: The author beside a heritage plaque on the building where she once lived.

Rooms 2, 4, and 6, which looked onto Peking Road, faced a four-story building with small apartments on its top floor. A German man by the name of Mr. Mueller lived there. He was repatriated to Germany right after the war. The other foreign resident was a hefty-looking Russian prostitute, who eventually died in the early '50s with no one to take care of her except the beggar who had slept under the stairs of the building for years, living on leftovers from the residents. On the second floor was the Indian Club, which flew its national flag whenever it held an event. Its long hallway was lined with tall windows and had iron fencing on its balcony, which faced Peking Road, where there was one entrance. Next to its entrance was another doorway that led to a second building, although the façade of both buildings was designed to look as though they were one. There has been little evident change to the surroundings of the CTC over the course of the past century. Nearly all of the neighbouring buildings have remained untouched, although for some reason, a tacky older building across the street is now known as the Ward Building. The only one that has been razed so far is the synagogue.

Our family consisted of my grandmother, my parents and myself. Originally, we all lived in a house in a typical Chinese residential lane in Hongkew called 春阳里 (Qun Yang Li, or Sunny Spring Lane). It was the only place my father knew as home, and was near St. Francis Xavier's, a school he attended from the age of twelve until he graduated and got a job working for Siemens on the ground floor of the Hardoon Building on Nanking Road. In the early 1930s, a few friends in the old neighbourhood moved into the International Settlement to be nearer to their jobs. My grandmother was reluctant to move because our old neighbourhood was home to her mahjong cronies. But when rumours of the Japanese threats to close the bridges across Soochow Creek to the International Settlement became so persistent, they all but verged on fact, we had no choice but to flee.

STARTING OVER

On August 13, 1937 (or perhaps a day or two before), my mother, who was several months pregnant with her second child at the time, carrying me on her back and holding tightly onto my grandmother, a woman who was prematurely old, with a large belly and chopstick-thin legs but who, thank goodness , did not have bound feet, joined the sea of refugees fleeing Hongkew on Garden Bridge.

I have seen a photo of the stampede and wondered if I'd be able to find us in a magnified version. I was 20 days short of being two and a half years old at the time, so I must have weighed a fair amount, and in addition to carrying me and making sure my grandmother didn't get swept away by the crowds, my mother was holding onto a white enamel bucket full of rice. This was how we made our way to our destination, 156 Peking Road, where some of our old neighbours had settled a few years before. We looked up Mr. Gu, who was the manager. After much haggling, he reluctantly gave us use of Room 6, the only vacant room on the second floor, but only after my grandmother paid three months' rent in silver dollars and Uncle Giles, a former Hongkew neighbour who lived in Rooms 16 and 17 on the second floor with his two wives and four children, acted as guarantor. He worked for The British American Tobacco Company (B.A.T.), which was just a short block away.

We later found out that our former home in Hongkew was looted and occupied by neighbours who knew that we would never return because my father's job was in the International Settlement. As it turned out, traffic was never actually cut between Hongkew and the International Settlement, however there were Japanese soldiers guarding every bridge across Soochow Creek, and Chinese men who had to cross were forced to bow to them. If the soldiers were displeased or just in a mood, pedestrians were detained and perhaps taken to Bridge House when the soldier left duty. Bridge House was a torture centre and few of those who were taken in survived the ordeal that awaited. That was something to be feared, especially when crossing Sichuan Road Bridge.

Life began from scratch in Room 6. Three months later, and thanks to a second addition, three generations of us were crammed into a room less than 12 square meters in size. The rooms on the second floor of 156 Peking Road were never meant to house families, who needed to cook three meals a day. We had to light our stoves early each morning on the balcony. Like nearly all stoves used by the other families, it burned briquettes for fuel. After the stove was lit, it was taken down and placed on a stool in the hallway just outside our room. All the other families did the same. When it was too hot, the stove would be placed on a low stool on the balcony. Hot and boiling water could be bought at a place across the street, and more than once a day, we'd have to go down with a big copper kettle to get hot water. In later years, we'd use buckets to get hot water for baths or sponge baths. Gas stoves were not installed until the early '80s.

When we moved into 156, Rooms 2 and 4 were occupied by a Cantonese physician called 陈炳威 (Chen Bingwei), a quack who referred to himself a general practitioner, his wife and child. One of the rooms was used as his office. Rooms 7, 8 and 10 were occupied by another physician who had studied in the U.S but who had had his license revoked when he botched an abortion for the daughter of a well-known Shanghai resident. This mishap forced him to change location, and by the time he reached 156, he was presenting himself as a doctor of venereal disease for men. Room 7, which had no windows, was his waiting-room, Room 8 was where he treated patients, and Room 10 was where he offered consultations. He did rather good business, and was helped by a close relative.

Room 12 was the office of a man who dealt in pharmaceuticals. Room 14 was occupied by an old lady whom we call 'ah paw' (grandma), whose daughter 梁爱莲 (Liang Ailian) was known to us as 'Auntie Ellen'. Her husband, Mr. So (苏) came from a family of consumptives. Auntie Ellen had vowed that she would only marry him once he was cured, but after more than a decade rolled by and she realized that there was no hope of his ever being healed, as his health was deteriorating rapidly, she reluctantly married him. They had two daughters, Alice and Bertha, shortly before he died. Alice was a year older than my sister Charlotte, who was born in 1943, and Bertha was a year younger. These two orphaned girls became almost like our own siblings.

Rooms 16 and 17 were the biggest on the floor. They were occupied by Uncle Giles. Despite his name, he was Cantonese and 100% Chinese. As the story went, his mother was a washerwoman who did the laundry for foreigners, one of whom was named Giles. When he found that she had a son, he generously offered to pay for his schooling, so the boy enrolled at St. Francis Xavier's and took Giles as his last name, and John as his first. Uncle Giles was at least twenty years my father's senior and was not able to read Chinese, although later we found out that his Chinese name was 蔡锦麒 (Cai Jinqi). After graduation, Uncle Giles worked for B.A.T. until his death shortly after Pearl Harbour.

His first marriage had been arranged, and he had no feelings whatsoever for his anaemic-looking Wife No. 1, who was hated by everyone. She was extremely mean, and the neighbours, all of whom were Cantonese, used to say that even a fertilized egg would not hatch if she had touched it. Wife No. 2 was the younger sister of a non-English-speaking colleague at B.A.T. whom he had gotten pregnant. The girl's mother had insisted that he marry her, as in those days men who could afford to had more than one wife, and there was no law against it. Wife No. 2 gave Giles his two eldest children, a daughter and a son, Frank 蔡华昌 (Cai Huachang). The daughter eloped with someone from French Town (which was what we always called the French Concession), and Uncle Giles had her legally disowned. Like his father, Frank also studied at Francis Xavier but learned Chinese at the same time. He later became a Catholic.

Several years later, Wife No.1 gave birth to two boys, Robert 蔡华德 (Cai Huade) and William 蔡华霖 (Cai Hualin) who also studied at the same school as Frank, and also learned Chinese. William was twelve years older than me. Since Robert was born in the Year of the Dog, he was known us as 狗哥哥 (Gou Ge Ge or Brother Dog), while William was known as 猪哥哥 (Zhu Ge Ge or Brother Pig), as he was born in the Year of the Pig, like me.

The family in Room 15, a couple and their daughter, was also Cantonese, and were former neighbours from Hongkew. Their Chinese family name was Li, but the father, who had been my father's classmate at SFX, became a Catholic and adopted the last name of his godfather, Gonsalves (or was it Consalves), who was Macanese, meaning he was Cantonese with Portuguese blood. Such people were referred to as 'hahm ha zhang' 咸虾撑 (xian xia cheng) by the Cantonese, meaning 'stuffed or gorged with salted shrimp paste', salted shrimp paste being a local product of Macao. He was also referred to as 矮仔 (ai zai, or 'shorty', to be polite), as he was no more than five feet tall.

After graduation Mr. Gonsalves bought a passport from a corrupt official at the Portuguese Consulate, found a job at a foreign bank as a Portuguese citizen, and got paid the foreign rate. He was unable to read Chinese. In those days, many Chinese with an English education preferred to be stateless than Chinese, and those with the means would buy foreign passports, though many were later revoked because they had been sold illegally by corrupt consular staff.

Rooms 18 and 19 did not have windows, as they had originally been storage rooms, but shortly after we moved in, a Toishanese family moved into Room 18. The Toishanese, like the Swatownese, are also from Guangdong Province, but have their own distinctive dialect which is different to Cantonese. The man did not work and depended on remittances from his father, who was a labourer in Canada. They had come from their home in Toishan in the hopes of joining the old man in Canada. But when the war broke out, that hope was dashed, and they were stranded in Shanghai, a city that spoke a dialect that to them was incomprehensible. They didn't even speak Cantonese, which was what the residents of the second floor spoke.

After the birth of my late sister Betty (1937-1986), there were five people in our small room. My parents' double bed took up nearly half the room, and the rest of the space was occupied by my grandmother's single bed, a small table, plus two camphor trunks, which were placed head-to-head with a quilt cover on top, on which I slept. Upon entering the room, you could immediately see all the way to the building across the street, and we used to say that it was like 'opening your mouth to see the lungs' (张开嘴巴看见肺, zhang kai zui ba kan jian fei).

During those early years, Rooms 7, 8, 10 and 12 and Rooms 1, 3 and 5 were closed after office hours as they were used by businesses, so the residents had the use of the hallway. Some put camp beds there so they need not sleep in their crowded rooms, especially when the weather was hot, or it wasn't too cold to sleep in the hall. However, those days didn't last long, as more people moved in each time a room was vacated. Room 9 was actually made up of two other rooms, 11 and 13, and was used as a dormitory by the single male employees of a small nearby department store.

One day a few months after we moved in, my parents took us to Uncle Jimmy's house on what used to be Avenue Victor Emmanuel, for a bath. It was just before Chinese New Year, and my grandmother had arranged to spend her day with some friends while we spent our day at Uncle Jimmy's. 'Uncle' Jimmy was actually James Pomeroy Hawes, a well-off Eurasian, and my mother had grown up there. When she was very young, she was left there by her 'aunt', who was either a Buddhist or a Taoist nun, and entrusted to the Hawes family, where she was effectively treated like a maid, just slightly better than one that had been hired. She learned to speak English, but never received an education in Chinese or in English and only left the house to marry when she was in her late twenties or early thirties. However, a genial relationship developed between our two families that lasted a lifetime.

While we were away for the day, the doctor in Rooms 2 and 4, a fellow Cantonese, pushed through the connecting door to our room, and ransacked the place, hoping to find something he could steal, thinking that we were rich because my parents dressed presentably. My father always went to work in suit and tie, and although he only had three or four shirts, he had half a dozen sets of collars and cuffs, which were changed every day, to be washed, starched, and ironed. They were attached using studs. He also had several pairs of cufflinks, hand-me-downs from Uncle Jimmy. My mother never went out without make-up and earrings, and her Chinese gowns were never made of cheap material.

When the rumours that the Japanese planned to close down the bridges across Soochow Creek first began to circulate, my mother had taken her valuables, including her diamond engagement ring, jade brooch, gold bracelet and ruby ring, to be placed in the safe at Uncle Jimmy's house, so the doctor found nothing. However, he did not have time to tidy up the mess he'd made because we returned before he could. Finding the place topsy turvy, we immediately knew who had broken in.

The doctor denied that it was him, saying that his room had also been broken into. But my mother, who was very feisty, called all the neighbours in to look at the mess, and none of them doubted that he had been responsible. Even though we did not end up losing anything, my mother shamed and nagged him publicly every chance she got, until he had no choice but to move to a house in Tengfeng Li, but we would still run into him now and then.

A FUNERAL, ACCORDING TO CANTONESE TRADITION

My mother was happy with our move to 156 Peking Road because it was nearer to people she considered family. She had spent thirty years or more with the Hawes, and their relatives— the Fords, the Johnstons, the Kays and the Wards—were people she had known while growing up in the Hawes household. However, my grandmother did not adjust well to the new surroundings because of the tight housing situation. She had always had her own room, but now she only had space for a single bed in a room she shared with her son, his wife and two children. At the end of 1939, that became three children, as she welcomed her first grandson.

My grandmother was in her mid-seventies at the time and had problems with her digestive system. She had to be interned at St Luke's Hospital, which was near the Holy Trinity Cathedral, and was there for quite a while before she died. Since we had no blood relatives in Shanghai, my parents were in a dither over the funeral arrangements. They had no choice but to call on my grandmother's former mahjong cronies for help, as well as on an elderly gentleman we called 'Granduncle' because he was a close friend of my Grandfather's, and had entrusted care of his wife and son to him in the event that he died, or else left for his home in Guangdong.

As an only child, my father had no one to share the expenses incurred by his mother's extended hospitalization and funeral. He had already been forced to begin from scratch after we moved from our old home in Hongkew. Now, with a wife and three children to support, as well as the unexpected sickness and death of his mother, his savings were almost gone. Life was not easy. According to Cantonese custom, the deceased is moved to a temple. Although my grandmother was not a practising Buddhist, she had paid a subscription to a Cantonese monk from the 国恩寺 (Guoen Temple) who visited her every month, so it was only natural that the funeral should be held there.

This is where funeral commemorations, known as the Sevenths, are held. There are seven in all, but it was often only the wealthy who were able to commemorate them all. On the first Seventh, mourners usually brought a satin 被面 (bei mian, or quilt cover) on which the names of the deceased and the gift giver was attached, along with a word of remembrance. The paper characters were either stuck on with paste, or pinned on with needles, so that the quilt was not damaged and could be used later for another funeral. They were never flashy, no reds or pinks, or glaring colours but usually silver-gray, pale blue, pale lavender or any other colour that did not create a 'wow'. The bei mian were hung around the coffin throughout the Sevenths.

With our finances dwindling, my father could only afford to commemorate three Sevenths. Custom also required the son to be unshaven during the mourning period, but as my father was working for a foreign company, which required its staff to be presentable and cleanshaven, he was not able to comply, and he was only present during the Sevenths on Sundays. The deceased is laid out in an open coffin which rests perpendicular to the altar, on which incense and candles are burned. Professional

Figure 3: The area's location makes it ripe for redevelopment. Credit: Dan Stein

mourners kneel at both ends of the altar and begin to cry on cue when a monk strikes a wooden fish to announce the arrival of someone who has come to pay their last respects.

Family members are also supposed to kneel near the altar but in my grandmother's case, my father was only able to attend on Sundays, and my mother was nursing her third child. My sister and I were much too young to keep still. The temple provided a vegetarian lunch and dinner, which all the friends and mahjong cronies thoroughly enjoyed, and they kept this 'show' running. After the third and (for us) the last Seventh ended, the coffin was sealed, and my grandmother's blood relatives (meaning my parents and the three of us) followed her coffin to the Cantonese Cemetery, dressed in white clothes and hemp.

Her death heralded others in our neighbourhood. Mr. So from Room 14 soon followed. He died of TB of the lungs, a family illness from which his younger brother and father also suffered. According to the practice at that time, a big pancake-like round of scrambled eggs was used to cover his face, to keep the TB from escaping. Immediately after he was taken to the funeral home, the official TB prevention office sent people to spray their room thoroughly, as well as to spray the hallway.

Then came the death of Mr. So's father, and after that, Dolly, one of the Li family daughters, who lived in Room 15, died of scarlet fever. She was only three or four years old and was their fourth daughter. Their eldest, Nancy, had died before I was born. Dolly's death left the Li's with two daughters, Norma, who was a year older than me, and another daughter who was a year younger. Dolly was considered 'remarkable', in that whenever she walked into a neighbour's room and saw something nice, she would say "we also have one, but ours is better than yours". Now, no child can be taught to say something like that—and Dolly was unfailing—it was just in her to up the ante.

A year or so later, Mrs. Li had another girl, Catherine, who lived less than a year. After that, the family had three boys, Francis, Freddie, and Edward. Since everyone at 156 had so little space, the doors to the rooms were never closed—at most a half-curtain was hung up, so every knew everybody else's business. By the time WWII began, and in spite of these deaths, the number of residents had actually increased because of newborns.

Although we were crowded into such limited space with so many children—and worse, a consumptive family and children dying of scarlet fever, meningitis and whatnot—like most Cantonese, we did not go to Western doctors because they were expensive. Any healthcare problems we had were taken care of by a Cantonese woman doctor of traditional Chinese medicine called Lum Geet Chew (林洁超), who had taken care of us at our former home. Dr. Lum would visit once every two weeks if anyone was sick, and once a month if there wasn't. She did not charge for her visits but wrote prescriptions to be filled at a Chinese medicine shop near Henning Road in Hongkew. Every prescription with her name on it would involve five to seven doses of different medicinal herbs, separately wrapped in individual packages, each with a tiny package of crab apple wafers 山楂片 (shan zha pian).

As children, we dreaded taking Chinese medicine, especially the first brew, and our mother would make us take a second brew, and sometimes even a third brew, to milk all the goodness out of the herbs. I still remember that we had a clay pot containing malt, and we were rewarded with a spoonful after a bowlful of the inevitably bitter medicine. A prescription would mean taking at least two or three bowls of bitter ooze each day for up to a month, but it must have worked, because we remained healthy, and none of us died.

Like many Cantonese, Dr. Lum left Shanghai for Hong Kong soon after Liberation. Her youngest daughter remained, however, and later got married and lived in an apartment in a building on Dixwell Road in Hongkew, but during one of the political movements in the early 1950s, both she and her husband committed suicide by putting their heads in a gas oven.

My father's association with the foreign community in Shanghai left our family with issues of our own. While the investigations into his past revealed nothing of any importance, the fact that we had been investigated at all was sufficient to complicate life. Consequently, I chose to relocate to Xinjiang in 1956, and while the situation there was not initially much better—I spent the first 16 years in Altay unemployed, and the relocation was hard on my husband—I was eventually able to make a place for myself.

Over the years, I have come to love Xinjiang. I never returned to Shanghai to live, but my memories of 156 have never left me, and remain as vivid as the day they were first made.

Margaret Sun now lives in an apartment on the University of Xinjiang campus in Urumqi, where she taught English for several decades. Her childhood home at 156 Peking Road in Shanghai still stands, although recently announced plans mean that it may not for very much longer. The CTC building's central location makes the blocks around it ripe for redevelopment. If it is demolished, the last traces of the lives it had once sheltered will live on in the memories, now recorded in this article, of an 88-year-old Cantonese woman in Urumqi.

FANS AND THE FLAMES: FANS DEPICTING FOREIGNERS IN TIENTSIN, 1858-1870

By Pierre-Henri Biger

ABSTRACT

The fan, an object that has always been widespread throughout the world, has been for centuries a special link between Chinese and European cultures. In this article, a few of these objects will illustrate the, unfortunately too often dramatic, evolution of relations between east and west in the 18th and 19th centuries.

HAND FANS FROM EAST TO WEST

The fan, an object to make wind for cooling off, fanning a fire, or hunting insects, existed, possibly as early as humans themselves, in the form of a leaf, a flat bone or feathers. Most civilisations have seen the development of fans, often as marks of dignity or social position. But these objects, with or without a handle, are generally 'fixed', and often called 'screens' in Europe. Europe had known folded fans in the shape of a cockade since antiquity, but it was in Asia (Japan, Korea, China) that folding and *brisés* fans[A] were born. They reached the west much later, not without interactions with India. It was the Portuguese who introduced these folding or *brisés* fans into Europe at the end of the 16th century, as evidenced by a few, rare surviving objects and portraits, such as those of Queen Elizabeth I of England. It took a century for the aristocracy of various countries, and in particular France, to show sufficient demand for these objects for the development of both local manufacture and tastes created by fashion. This brought European merchants to make increasingly precise requests of Chinese craftsmen, through the various companies specialising in this trade.

The desire of Chinese craftsmen to respond to this demand led to the creation of objects intended for the western market, the best known being the fans often called in Europe 'Mandarins', or 'one hundred faces', exported mainly from Canton or Macau. From the

---

A   Folding fan: A type of fan with pleated leaf, the leaf being the paper or fabric part of this object (T'zu shan). *Brisé* fan: English term (using a French word) for a leafless fan composed of overlapping sticks, wider on the upper portion and held together by a silk thread or ribbon (Hu shan).

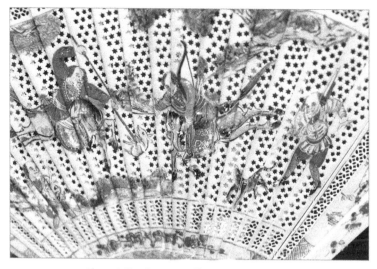

Figure 1: Hunting scene with westerners circa 1715

Figure 2: Moses and the Daughters of Jethro, recto

end of the 17th century, certain fans show an interesting meeting of cultures and it is these, taken from the author's own collection, we will discuss here. Thus, a *brisé* fan from the reign of Kangxi and the end of the reign of Louis XIV, Figure 1, shows a hunting scene with westerners recognisable for their breeches and black square-toed shoes.[1]

Later in the 18th century, a beautiful European leaf shows a biblical scene, *Moses and the Daughters of Jethro*, after Francesco de

Mura, mounted on a remarkable ivory *monture*[B], Figure 2, with a very interesting ornamental hybridisation.[2] It mixes typically Chinese motifs: the bat symbol of chance, chrysanthemums, asters, simulated jades but also shells, falling vines and flowers and rococo motifs that are entirely European, although mixed with dragon heads. This mixture of cultures makes it possible to satisfy the European taste for exoticism without, however, disorienting it. This will result, as in other sectors of the market, in the production by English or French fan makers of *chinoiserie* fans. But in China, the same goal will sometimes lead to significant or humorous errors. Thus, a fan from the end of the 18th century has on its recto a leaf copying, in a rather clumsy way, a pastoral by François Boucher (1703-1770) but on the verso a landscape and two Chinese characters are painted, very probably by a Chinese artist, in the European style.[3] The mother-of-pearl *monture,* Figure 3, is treated in a characteristically Chinese manner, engraved rather than carved, with European motifs, like ships, but sometimes misunderstood or distorted by the craftsman. One can only smile when seeing the profile of a European man, shown with an exaggeratedly long nose!

Another fan, Figure 4, no doubt made (as was the previous one) for one of the India companies, offers on the front of its leaf a historical scene, probably *The Continence of Scipio*, but with features (including long noses) or imperfections coming from the faulty copy by the Chinese painter of a European engraving.[4] Clearly these imperfections are understandable: how could an artist from Canton have imagined the uniforms of Roman soldiers? But the mother-of-pearl *montures* are

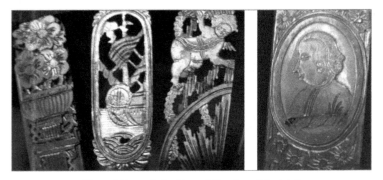

Figure 3: Pastoral after François Boucher, sticks detail

B   A *monture* (French word also used in English) comprises the ensemble of the sticks, including the two outer sticks, usually stouter, which are named *guards*.

Figure 4: An historical scene mixing European and Chinese styles

typical of Chinese work, and the verso of the leaf shows Mediterranean landscapes, but interpreted by a local brush, and embellished with wholly Asian scenes. At the same time, the fashion for *chinoiseries* that flourished in the west probably produced many fans which, seen from Beijing, could only arouse the same smiles or laughter.

Two Tientsin Treaty Fans 1858

Despite these artistically dreamed-up worlds, the encounters between Europe and China in the 17th and 18th centuries remained essentially commercial, even if there were controversies, notably religious, arising from the intrusion into a world quasi-autonomous for millennia by representatives of a distant culture. It was, however, during the 19th century that these relations took on a character which continues two hundred years later to mark international relations. In this context the production of Chinese fans for the European or American markets developed considerably, mainly from Canton. A few rare fans testify in a singular way to the confrontations of this period. We have neither the skill, nor the desire to broach delicate political questions here, but it is necessary to situate the three objects that we are going to study.

The first two relate to what is known as the Second Opium War (1856-1860) when Britain and France, followed less actively but opportunistically by the United States and Russia, engaged in disproportionate reprisals following the capture on 8 October 1856 of the Arrow, a Chinese ship flying the British flag, and the torture and death in February 1856 of a missionary, Father Auguste Chapdelaine.[5] It is obvious that the western powers saw in these

Figure 5: Allied gunboats on the Peiho, 1858, recto

events an opportunity to obtain new commercial advantages from the Emperor of China, after those granted by the Treaty of Nanjing in 1842. It was in this context that the British and French fleets attacked and occupied Canton at the end of 1857, before moving towards Tientsin, attacking the forts of Dagu. The Chinese had to resolve to sign, in June 1858, the Treaties of Tientsin with Lord Elgin, commander of the British troops, and with General Baron Gros, commander of the French forces.

Figure 5 shows the first of two fans from this time, a fan with a *monture* of black lacquered, bamboo guards and painted green sticks. It measures 30.6 cm. The double leaf, in paper 18 cm wide, is printed and gouached on the recto, decorated on the verso with flakes of painting and green sinuosities. The recto shows houses supporting two flags, one tricolour and obviously French. In front is a steamer with paddle wheels, two funnels, two masts and several guns. It is joined by a rowboat with five rowers. Both ships fly a British flag, red with a white quarter crossed with blue.

What scene is depicted here? It turns out that an identical fan, but with red lacquered sticks and Chinese characters on the guards, belongs to the collections of the *Musée d'Art et d'Histoire* of La Rochelle, France. This fan, unfortunately in rather poor condition, was donated to this museum in 1871 by the Baron de Chassiron (1818-1871). The Martin de Chassiron family is one of the most famous families of Charente-

Maritime, a *département* in southwestern France. It counts among its members eminent navigators, travellers, diplomats, politicians, and men of letters. Baron Charles-Gustave de Chassiron participated from 1858 to 1860 in a diplomatic mission sent to the Far East to renew commercial relations with China and Japan. He brought back from this mission an important collection of books and everyday objects. At the end of 1861, he published his travel diary in which he recounted his marvellous discovery of Far Eastern Asia. Among his purchases, one finds very diverse objects: lacquers, works of marquetry and worked bamboos, ivories, carved wood, sabres, books, coins of gold and silver. Among these objects were two Chinese fans, the one described here, and another that will be discussed later. On the verso of this fan, handwritten inscriptions in French, obviously written by Chassiron himself, appears:

> Les canonnières alliées dans le Peho (pour les Chinois)
> Allied gunboats in the Peho (for the Chinese)

> Tien Tsin près Pékin-Juillet 1858 (mission de Chine)
> Tien Tsin near Beijing-July 1858 (mission of China)

Charles-Gustave de Chassiron published in 1861 his *Notes sur le Japon, la Chine et l'Inde*, which verify that he was indeed present in Tientsin in July 1858, shortly after the signing of the treaty. As the gunboat represented bears the British flag, we can assume that, as Baron de Chassiron speaks of 'allied gunboats', it was for the author of this leaf a symbolic representation of British and French ships, although not a representation that was very consistent with reality. We have yet to find a western image corresponding to this gunboat with two funnels;

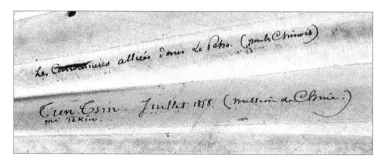

Figure 6: Allied gunboats on the Peiho, 1858, verso

however this print is close to representations made by local artists of gunboats, but as far as we know with a single funnel.⁶

What are the buildings that we see on the shore? The Baron de Chassiron speaks of them in a letter to M. de La Gueronnière reproduced in his *Notes*:

> During their stay in Tien-Tsin, the Ambassadors of France and England lived in a vast wooden palace, like all the palaces in China, which is called *yamoun*: I found them there. They shared it among themselves, keeping around them, camped rather than housed, their respective staffs scattered in the many kiosks which form the interior layout of any large Chinese dwelling. Part of the English Mission was lodged in a pagoda annexed to the main *yamoun*, and whose courtyard, planted with centuries-old trees, was covered by a velum which made it a place that was always cool. [...] Our Mission lived, in the middle of trees and artificial rocks, in the kiosks of a garden which had to be tended at the time when the Emperor Kien-Long received, in this same *yamoun*, Lord Amherst, the English envoy, who worthily refused humiliating demands of etiquette, at the *Ko-tou*, that eternal obstacle to our diplomatic relations with the very person of the Emperor of China.⁷

Alfred, Marquis de Moges (1830-1861), was part of the French delegation when the Tientsin treaties were signed, and on the premises before Chassiron. He wrote his *Souvenirs d'une ambassade en Chine et au Japon en 1857 et 1858* ⁸ which were, for the large part, reproduced the same year with illustrations by Gustave Doré after designs or watercolours by M. de Trévise, another member of the delegation.⁹ In this book we find an illustration showing the same buildings we see on these fans.¹⁰ Mqs. de Moges specifies:

> It is there that rises the *yamoun* that the two ambassadors have chosen for their residence. Lord Elgin occupies the left side, and Baron Gros the other half. This *yamoun*, quite degraded, was built by Emperor Kien-Foung, one of the ancestors of the current emperor, who had made it

his summer residence, as various inscriptions still visible attest.[11]

The illustration, complemented by de Moges and Chassirons' writings, makes it obvious that the buildings shown on the fan we study are indeed, although represented in a simplistic way, those of this *yamoun* or palace. A necessary question remains: under what conditions were those printed fans made, one of them being certainly bought on the spot in July 1858 by the Baron de Chassiron? Certain notes by the Marquis de Moges may give an answer for he specifies that 'all the commercial activity seems to have been concentrated in the suburbs, especially in the one which runs along the Grand-Canal. It is there that one finds the shops of furs, wallpapers, fans, and the rare antiques that Tientsin can offer to the curiosity of the foreigner' but also:

Figure 7: A caricature portrait of two Europeans

We see some caricatures at our address, which the Chinese hastily make disappear as we pass; but, seeing that we only laugh at them, they then show them to us and let us take them away. There is a grotesquely decked out European who haggles over a hedgehog and ends up buying it for a big bag of cash. Then an English officer, on horseback, holding his white umbrella in one hand, and having a cigar in his mouth, with impossible hat and bearing. We give them some European drawings for which they are very eager, and the next day we find these drawings reproduced and having already taken on a grotesque appearance.

If the representation of the gunboat and the *yamoun* do not present this 'grotesque' character, another fan brought back by Chassiron, Figure 7, which he offered to the Musée de La Rochelle corresponds perfectly to this description. On this fan, completely painted and not printed like the previous one, we see, mounted on two small horses, typical of the region, two Europeans, characterised by untidy red beards and white trousers, equipped with whips. One wears a white hat, perhaps a reinterpreted tropical helmet, the other a (sailor's?) cap and a jacket with shoulder pads and a sword at his side. The guards of the black lacquered bamboo fans present engravings in Chinese, that we suppose unrelated; but on the back, an inscription again most likely by Chassiron's hand indicates: 'Les Anglais dans la ville (pour les Chinois) (The English in the city [for the Chinese])' and 'Tien-Tsin près Pékin—Juillet 1858 (mission de Chine) (Tien-Tsin near Beijing-July 1858 [Chinese mission])'. Although the object was in the hands of a Frenchman, and not an Englishman, one can imagine that these illustrations were caricatural portraits made on demand, as many artists currently offer in the tourist sites of many countries. The making of such objects in Tientsin should not come as a surprise as we know that many popular prints were produced in Yangliuqing, a suburb of Tientsin, especially New Year pictures which appeared around the reign of Emperor Wanli (1573–1620) in the Ming Dynasty, or pictures of the *zhima* type.[12]

Nonetheless, it seems clear that local craftsmen took advantage of the presence of foreigners to produce, in 1858 essentially for them, instant souvenir objects, with a somewhat caricatural character but sufficiently moderate to make both natives and Europeans smile, and to justify a purchase.[13] This is testimony to the ingenuity, artistic talents, and business acumen of the local people.

THE TIENTSIN 1870 MASSACRE FAN

The third fan that we want to study has, alas, a more dramatic character, but is completely related to the two previous ones, as much by the way it is made as by the location of the scene shown and by the illustration it gives of the evolution of the relations between local authorities and Europeans under the influence of the 'unequal treaties', including that of Tientsin. This one, Figure 8, appears in two copies in the author's collection but has not yet been encountered in public collections, perhaps for lack of sufficient identification.

This fan is 30cm long [11.8 inches] including 17cm [6.7 inches] for the leaf. The sticks are bamboo, and the leaf is made of local paper, possibly rice. The rivet also is traditional. The head is square, and if the leaf is closed, when viewed from the side it has a concave arc. The leaf is printed and painted in watercolour and gouache. At first glance, the crude colours somewhat hide the details of the scenes, but we will see that that was perhaps desired by the fan maker.

This fan has been reproduced by Prof. Robert Bickers in his book *The Scramble for China*,[14] and illustrates his text explaining the events which are so recorded.[15] What do we see on this fan? Many are seen in front of a burning, twin-spired church and other buildings, some

Figure 8: The Tientsin 1870 Massacre Fan

Figure 9: The Tientsin 1870 Massacre Fan as illustrated in *Every Saturday—An Illustrated Journal of Choice Reading*

sharing this fate. On the church, Chinese characters can be seen. Several Chinese men, exhorted by a Mandarin descended from his chair, sword in hand, attack westerners, at least two of whom are lying on the ground. On the other side of a river and on a boat, other Chinese people are preparing to intervene.

When my wife and I found this fan, we were very happy as we immediately recognised it as a fan which had been shown in an article in *Every Saturday—An Illustrated Journal of Choice Reading*, published in Boston, Massachusetts, on 24 December 1870[15]. That fan is shown without the added painting and is therefore more clearly readable. One soon understands that it is not a peaceful landscape: a church on fire, numerous armed people attacking some others. The legend sheds light on the subject.

The article on page 838 of *Every Saturday* provides a clear and concise summary of the events.

> The picture of a fan on page 837 possesses a painful interest, though the fan itself is grotesque enough to make one smile in spite of all. Immediately after the Tientsin massacre of the 21st June, many thousands of these fans were manufactured for the purpose of notifying throughout the Empire the terrible event which had recently taken place in that city. The foreigners resident at the settlement naturally fearing that the sight of this pictorial representation might

stimulate the natives to further deeds of bloodshed and violence, remonstrated through their official authorities with Chung-How, the Governor of Tientsin, begging him to stop the circulation of these inflammatory missives. He at once complied with this request, but by the time his prohibition was put in force many thousands of these fans had been dispersed throughout the country.

The fan represents the burning of the Roman Catholic Cathedral, together with the French consulate, and the massacre of the foreigners. On the left a Mandarin has risen from his chair, and is urging the people to vengeance. Close to him the French Consul is being brutally murdered. The bridge of boats opposite was not allowed to be opened by Tseng Kwoh-Swai, the great promoter of the massacre. According to many accounts, Chung-How wished to open this bridge, so as to prevent the people from crossing the river, but he was not able to effect his object, so that after the populace had done all the mischief they could, they crossed, and finished their brutal work by torturing and murdering those unfortunate Sisters of Charity, who had been so good and kind to them all, setting fire to the place, and throwing them among the burning embers. The foreign residents were, no doubt, right in regarding the circulation of the fan as mischievous, but we scarcely think they were justified in assuming that they were manufactured with the direct aim of encouraging further outrages. We rather incline to regard them as a primitive mode of circulating a piece of startling news.

Although this *Every Saturday* article gives quite an accurate relation of the facts, further explanations may be helpful. Why such a violence against Europeans and against priests and nuns? The resentment, against mainly Britain and France, was understandable after the Opium Wars and the treaties opening more and more places in China to European and U.S businessmen, and especially after the sacking of the Imperial Summer Palace in October 1860. But why such hostility against Christians? We must remember the 1st Treaty of Tientsin, the occasion for the issuance of the fans shown earlier, between France and China, other treaties being signed with Britain, the USA and

Russia. It states, in Article 13:

> The Christian religion having for essential purpose to bring the men to virtue, members of all Christian communities will enjoy full security for their people, their properties and the free exercise of religious practices; and an effective protection will be given to the missionaries who will go peacefully inside the country.

Alas, not only was the Christian faith in most places highly different from the local culture, but the missionaries were too closely linked with the foreign armies that were, logically, considered invaders. Robert Bickers quotes the Duke of Somerset, former First Lord of the Admiralty: 'The fact is [...] we are propagating Christianity with gunboats'.[16] In Tientsin, the clash began, it seems, with an altercation between a crowd and Chinese converts, which led the French Consul, Henri Fontanier, to complain to the Superintendent Chong Hou, and 'drunk with rage', to make use of a pistol, with no other result than getting himself, and many others, killed.

So, why did the Chinese mob torture and kill the nuns and the priests? Let us again quote Robert Bickers:

> [...] everybody knew this: they [the foreigners] gouged out Chinese eyes and used them to make medicine with; they used Chinese hearts for the same purpose. So they needed Chinese bodies [...] and established orphanages and children's homes, tricking people into placing children in their care, and there in those homes the children were killed'.[17]

What is the Roman Catholic version? We shall here use a book written by a French missionary, Maurice Collard.[18] It appears that a Lazarist Chinese priest, Father Joseph Tsiou, a skilled doctor, began the Roman Catholic mission in Tientsin. 'He specialises in the baptism of dying babies' [sic]. He met strong opposition from a part of the population before dying of illness in August 1861. He was replaced by another French missionary and by a group of nuns sent by the Congregation of the Daughters of Charity. Most of them were French, except for one Irish and one Belgian sister.

These nuns came, of course, with the best of intentions in both mind and heart: saving the souls of many Chinese from the Devil and from barbarism! That is why they continued, as their predecessor did, to baptise children on the brink of death: 'From the first year […] we could send six hundred little angels to heaven' wrote Sister Dutrouilh. But very quickly, some Tientsin inhabitants were suspicious of their activity, and at the end of 1863, Sister Martha says: 'Thousands of fabulous rumours run on our behalf, and the Christians here are too small a number to refute them'. After the purchase of a new house from a Mandarin, things seemed to improve a bit: 'The pagans are beginning to understand that we are not coming here to tear their eyes, or to make a trade advantage'. Note that 'the day of the killings [was] to be found […] a jar of pickled onions, and the people claimed that it was a can of eyes torn from children'.

The sisters were soon assisted by two Catholic Lazarist priests, one French, Claude-Marie Chevrier, appointed in late 1864 after a mission in Mongolia and the other Chinese, Vincent Ou.[19] In line with a charity then in vogue, the so-called 'Holy Childhood', they too sought to baptise and to teach young children, sometimes sick or stunted, whose families were unable or unwilling to keep them. In this strange exchange, the Chinese families were discharged of, often, sick or infirm children they could not afford to keep at home, and the nuns and priests could be convinced they had saved souls from the Devil. Father Chevrier, a former soldier, insisted on giving his church the name of 'Our Lady of Victories'. This was, perhaps, not such a good move psychologically.

But let us go back to some close-ups of the fan. On the left, Figure 10a, we are witnessing the beginning of the carnage; a Mandarin, descended from his palanquin, seems to incite the mob to violence. It is probably the French Consul Fontanier who is shown down beside this sedan chair, near the door of the church. Let us recall that as he

Figure 10a and 10b: Details from the Tientsin 1870 Massacre Fan

advocated, too late, for the threatened nuns, he shot at Superintendent Chong Hou, killing one of his servants. In front of the church, which is already in flames, must be the murder of M. Simon, Chancellor of the Consulate. Note the Chinese characters on the lintel of the door: we have been told that they simply mean "Church of God".

At bottom right, Figure 10b, the fan shows the 'bridge of boats' connecting the two sides of the river which allowed the mob, after having murdered the Consul of France, Chancellor Simon, Mr and Mrs Thomassin and Fathers Chevrier and Ou, to go to the house of the nuns (Jen-tang-t'se) to perform even more horrific deeds. It seems that, '…the Imperial High Commissioner, eager to save the adoptive mothers of the orphans, would have given the order to open the bridge, cutting off the cut-throats of the road to [...] Jen-tang t'sé. But he lacked the necessary energy, so when General Tchen-Kouo-Joei, after a moment contemplating the dock fire, led his hordes back [...] nobody dared to resist him.'[20]

The massacres were immediately condemned by the Chinese authorities. But we see in their reactions a reluctance that we understand, as the Celestial Empire was more than worried at being occupied by foreigners and being the victim of abuses such as those committed in the Imperial Summer Palace ten years earlier. Maurice Collard goes on,

> As soon as 25 June appeared an edict of the Emperor, condemning the heinous act, which directed the Vice-King and the Imperial Commissioner to conduct an investigation. Nothing is truly done, however, to apprehend the culprits, and so fifteen days over, they could walk with high foreheads and boast of their shameful deeds that without any shame, they had got painted on fans.

This fan is thus an act of political propaganda under the guise of disseminating information and was most certainly made to maintain a spirit of resistance against western 'devils'—mixing neatly, as did the rioters, the representatives of state and religion. The fact that the fan represents the murder of the Consul of France near the door of the church, clearly designated by the only Chinese characters on the fan, seems to be part of a well-concerted 'marketing plan'. This dramatic event remained long in the memory of the Catholic Church but has been forgotten by most French because of its occurrence at the same time as the outbreak of the disastrous 1870 war between France and Germany. When Chinese diplomats came to make amends, they bowed toward M. Alphonse Thiers, head of a state which was not yet the Third Republic, regretting the death of a Consul who represented the former Emperor Napoleon III, now exiled. The development in France during the following decades of anticlerical policies, may too have helped people to more or less forget this event.

These three fans, in our opinion, testify about the way foreigners were seen in Tientsin in the period 1860-1870. Is it not possible to see an evolution of the general mood? In 1858, the foreigners, although not totally welcome, were seen as strange and somewhat amusing people, who could be a source of financial income. Twelve years later, the same foreigners, and maybe especially the missionaries, seem to fully be *persona non grata*.

In a way, these fans and this evolution would correspond to the Chinese temperament as described by Paul Claudel.[21]

> Le Chinois, sous une apparence hilare et polie, est dans le fond un être fier, obstiné, malin, indépendant, incompressible et, somme toute, un des types humains les plus sympathiques et les plus intelligents que j'aie connus (sans préjudice des crises de folie furieuse, ce qu'on appelle là-bas la "ventrée de you".) Allons, à ta santé, vieux frère, homme libre ! Je t'aime bien !
>
> The Chinese, under a hilarious and polite appearance, is basically a proud, stubborn, clever, independent, incompressible being and, all in all, one of the most sympathetic and intelligent human types I have known (without prejudice to the fits of furious madness, what they call over there the "belly full of *you*".) So, cheers, old brother, free man! I like you!

After Fontanier's death in 1870, the city of Tientsin had other Consuls of France, among them the same Paul Claudel, a most famous diplomat, catholic writer and poet, who must have often thought of the Massacre of Tientsin when writing his *Cent phrases pour* éventails (*Hundred phrases for fans*). One of those phrases could serve as a conclusion:

Chut ! Si nous faisons du bruit, le temps va recommencer.
Hush! If we make noise, time will start again.

CONCLUSION

Objects may sometimes say more than witnesses do. The few fans described in this article, and many others, give, in our opinion, an idea of how the relationship between China and Europe evolved during the 18th and 19th centuries. At first, this encounter was accompanied by astonishment and interest in the discovery of physical and cultural differences and reinforced on both sides by the inevitable search for financial profits. But this contact between two hegemonic civilizations, European forces being at this time stronger, evolved later into incomprehension, and violence. The author of this article hopes that, in the future, hand fans will rather show understanding, mutual respect, and a desire for peace.

Pierre-Henri Biger (born 1951) after Law and Sciences Po Paris studies, Pierre-Henri worked in the mortgage and real estate sector. An amateur historian of antique fans, and a member of dedicated associations: Fan Circle International, Fan Association of North America, Cercle de l'Éventail, Friends of the Greenwich Fan Museum, he created the Place de l'Éventail website in 1998 (www.eventails.net). Once retired and after a Master's degree in History of Art, he defended in 2015 his PhD thesis Sens et sujets de l'éventail européen de Louis XIV à Louis-Philippe, *available online <https://www.theses.fr/2015REN20026>*

He has spoken about fans in various colloquia and conferences and has published numerous articles on the subject. He and his wife regularly lend fans to museums. He hopes to show that the hand fan, present in Europe from the 17th to the 21th century, is not only objet d'art *but also an excellent means of studying artistic and social history.*

We are grateful to Mélanie Moreau, Director of the La Rochelle Musées D'Art et D'Histoire for permission to use the images in Figures 6 and 7. These images show fans from their collection.

—∞—

REFERENCES

1. Brigitte Nicolas, *Un brin de panache*, Musée de la Compagnie des Indes, (Port-Louis, 2019), p. 38-39.

2. Nicolas, p. 70-71.
3. Nicolas, p. 68-69.
4. Nicolas, p. 62-63.
5. Canonised in 2000 by Pope John Paul II. This canonisation was strongly contested by the Chinese authorities, who still accuse the missionary of various crimes.
6. For instance, see on the internet, <the Farsham creek engagement in the Canyon River—From a Chinese drawing>, as published in 1857 by the *Illustrated London News*.
7. Charles de Chassiron, *Notes sur le Japon, la Chine et l'Inde*, (Paris, E. Dentu, 1861), p. 198.
8. M. de Moges, 'Voyage en Chine et au Japon 1857-1858', *Le tour du monde—Nouveau journal des voyages*, Edouard Charton Ed., (L. Hachette et Cie, Paris, 1860), p. 129-176.
9. de Moges, p. 149.
10. de Moges, p. 150.
11. Cf. Christophe Comendale, 'L'image populaire chinoise et la lune', *Actes du Colloque Papiers, Images, Collections, Le Vieux Papier*, Fascicule 358, Octobre 2000, Paris, p. 151-168., p. 152.
12. Pierre-Henri Biger, 'The Tianjin Massacre Fan'" *FANA Journal*, Fan Association of North America, Spring 2010, p. 10-16.
13. Robert Bickers, *The Scramble for China: Foreign Devils in the Qing Empire, 1832-1914* (Allen Lane, London, 2011), Figure. 14.
14. *Every Saturday—An Illustrated Journal of Choice Reading*, published in Boston, Massachusetts, on 24 December 1870.
15. Bickers, p. 232-235.
16. Bickers, p. 240.
17. Bickers, p. 230.
18. Maurice Collard, *Les martyrs de Tien-Tsin*, (Imprimerie de Balan-Sedan, Balan, 1926).
19. Jeremiah Jenne, 'Warrior Priest: The Mission of Claude-Marie Chevrier (1821-1870)', *Journal of the Royal Asiatic Society China*, Vol. 82 No. 1, 202, p. 69-88.
20. Collard, p. 155.
21. Paul Claudel, *Choses de Chine (1936)*, included in Œuvre *en prose*, Paris, Gallimard, (La Pléiade), 1965, p. 1024-1025.

SECTION 2

Annals and Archives

FLORENCE, AGAIN: A LIBRARIAN'S ARCHIVE BECKONS

BY FIONA LINDSAY SHEN

Eleven years ago, I wrote a book about Florence Ayscough's life in Shanghai, from her birth in the city in 1875, through the years she served as librarian for the North China Branch of the Royal Asiatic Society, to her departure for Canada in 1923.[1] After sailing out of Shanghai, though, she wasn't finished with China, flourishing as a sinologist, translator, art collector, writer, and passionate advocate for her country of birth until her death in Chicago in 1942.

And she wasn't finished with me. While I lived in China, she had been my guide to the landmarks of Shanghai. Browsing in the old Bibliotheca Zikawei, I would stumble across her signature and a few words of dedication in purple ink in books she donated to the library, or to other writers such as Lin Yutang. Those elegantly penned words felt like short notes to me across the decades. So many times, I paced the site of her Chinese courtyard home at 72 Penang Road (now Anyuan Road) near the northern border of the former International Settlement. In vain I scoured the urban streetscape at the back of the Jade Buddha Temple for remnants of her azalea-covered rockery, her waterfall, the paulownia and magnolia trees, a prized aged pine like 'a Buddhist priest or a Daoist,' or even, at my feet, a glittering shard of the turquoise tile she salvaged from the ruins of the Yuanmingyuan, sacked by British and French troops in 1860. She was my companion, mentor, and friend. The person who helped me feel more at home in a disorientating city. Mawkish as it may sound, I fell in love with her.

Like Florence, I moved from China to North America for family reasons. Her husband, Francis, was seriously ill; my children wanted to resume school in their birth country. We both picked the ocean. Florence settled at first in New Brunswick in the house built by her father overlooking the Bay of Fundy; I settled in the milder climes of southern California on the lip of a canyon that drops to the Pacific. Seventy miles inland from my home is the University of Redlands, a bucolic campus founded in the early 20th century on a vineyard, cradled by folded hills and orange groves. Alma Mater of Florence's second husband, Harley Farnsworth MacNair, its archives hold a large collection of the couple's papers, including much primary material relating to Florence. Sprawling over decades, encompassing private and professional correspondence, photographs, working papers, and ephemera, it is a historian's dream. Years after leaving Shanghai, browsing these letters and photographs is like settling in for a comfortable reunion with a beloved friend over a bottle or two of Californian pinot noir.

'What is the next sweet attention which you can possibly find to bestow upon a *vieux grognard* like me?' asks esteemed sinologist Herbert A. Giles, in a letter thanking her for an 80th birthday present.[2] Well, for a start, among all these unexpected treasures is a studio photograph of her dapper father and fashionable mother as newlyweds. So this is the young face of the founder of the eminently successful Shanghai Tug and Lighter Company! And here is a 1903 photograph of the spacious three-storey home with wrap-around verandas that was built for her and her first husband Francis Ayscough on Gordon Road (now Jiangning Road). In another folder I find this home's annotated floorplans and learn it was designed by Dowdall and Moorhead. (The Ayscoughs were obviously doing well—the Scottish architect William Dowdall, who set up practice in Shanghai in 1883, was the architect of Union Church on Suzhou Road, and later St. Ignatius Cathedral in Xujiahui.) I find photographs of a toddler in an extravagant sunbonnet in the Ayscoughs' garden—Florence's small nephew 'Tom-Tom Wheelock'. And Tom-Tom's father, Florence's brother Geoffrey, in a horse-drawn carriage rounding the gravel path to the house. Both Florence and Francis Ayscough were keen gardeners. I'm gratified to find a photograph of five Chinese gardeners weeding in the foreground—a simple acknowledgement of the human labor required to maintain these extravagant western edifices.

I dip into conversations begun a century ago. 'Do you remember asking me the Chinese name for the golden oriole, as to which I had to confess discreditable ignorance,' writes Reginald Fleming Johnston, a few years before he was appointed tutor to the last emperor, Puyi. 'There are golden orioles in the woods of the very temple in which I am now staying...I remember two years ago finding the wooded mountains of Chekiang (especially 天目山 [Tianmushan]) a very favourite haunt of the golden oriole.'[3]

There is a plaintive missive from Mr. Woo, the RAS assistant librarian: 'I should be much grateful to you, if you would kindly get me extra works that may be done at night time, as my present income ($60) is not enough for my expenses. I have been employed by the R.A.S. for twenty years and am extremely sorry to say that I have used up in these five years all the money which I saved in former years, as I spent $500 for my mother's funeral and $1000 for my son's marriage and also spent a good deal of money for expenses of medicines, as my wife and I have frequently been attacked by evil spirits in late years.'[4]

There are ephemera that gladden a historian's heart—envelopes from the 1920s postmarked Shanghai; handwritten asides on letters and articles; a few pieces of Florence's exquisite personal notepaper sprinkled with metallic pine needle fascicles (a reference to *Fir-Flower Tablets*, her first book of poetry translations co-authored with Amy Lowell); an engraved copper printing plate of the announcement of Florence's second marriage to MacNair in 1935 following Francis' Ayscough's death in 1933.

Her friendship and professional partnership with the American poet Amy Lowell and their joint translations of classical Chinese poetry were documented in their published letters.[5] But here in the Redlands archives are Florence's working papers. The penciled deliberations, questions, changes of heart, and asides about other scholars convince us we are touching a writer's mind. In China, Florence relied heavily on her Chinese teacher Nung Chu for help translating specific characters. The reams of calligraphy better than hers, with her penciled notes in the margins, persuade me I'm watching over their shoulders as they struggle to pin down the precise yet most poetic meaning for each individual character.

And there are, at last, solutions to mysteries. Back when I was writing my book about her, I was perplexed that her first husband Francis was named as the author of an imaginative essay 'Phantasmagoria,' published in 1929 in the East Asian Journal (*Ostasiatische Zeitschrift*). It is an extraordinary piece of micro speculative fiction, an early 'Night at the Museum,' inspired by a landmark exhibition of Chinese art in Berlin in 1929. In it, the works on exhibit, far removed from their gravesites and original collections, speak into the dark gallery. The tableau begins with a Shang dynasty ritual wine vessel on loan from a collector in Britain: 'The rams spoke first, those grave beasts who, standing back to back, support on their pearly haunches the vessel which once held sacred spirit made from grain: "We, the trustworthy, who stored the sacred wine, now look out through mists which rise from the river Thames. Our wine vessel is empty, but we will bear unflinching through ages to come the grave responsibility laid upon us by those who cast our forms three thousand years ago.'" Another bronze wine-pouring vessel rattles its shiny spines and consoles itself that now young visitors listen when it speaks 'of rites long dead, of reverence, of an indissoluble link with men'. A bronze bell acknowledges it has 'exchanged the burning loess plains for the long cold snow', while a Ming dynasty handscroll shakes the fragrance of plum blossom into the huge space which had been a gallery wall.⁶

Francis Ayscough, though, was an unlikely author of this piece. A successful British businessman employed by Scott, Harding and Co, Master of the Paper Hunt Club, and a pillar of his Shanghailander community, he had, by the time this article was published in 1929, been in poor health and had spent stretches of time in European sanatoria and hospitals. I had long been dubious that he, not his sinologist wife, Florence, had written this essay. And now, here in California, my doubt was rewarded. On an offprint of the article Florence has penned a note in her characteristic purple ink: 'To Mary S. From Florence A., written for Dr. Otto Kümmel [first director of the Royal Prussian Museums] after visiting the exhibition with him our viewing after everyone had gone.' And beside Francis' name on the offprint is Florence's salty aside to her friend: 'Did you know that Francis had turned author?!'⁷

One of my intentions in writing my book about Florence was to amplify the achievements of this woman writer at a time when the spotlight was trained on male translators such as Arthur Waley and Witter Bynner. To return even a short essay to its rightful author (instead of her husband) feels another small step towards acknowledging the work of Florence and the female writers, artists, and scholars like her who were dedicated to sharing Chinese culture with English-speaking audiences.

Speaking of her, I always remained unsure just how to pronounce her surname. A young child's letter from 1923 in this archive has at last put me straight: 'My darling Mrs. Assko. Thank you so much for the lovely bole and jug. I am going to Canada with you. When will I come? My birthday is on the 1 of December. I go to school. Love from Dick.'

I haven't finished with this archive, or with Florence. I have a fulltime job and two other books to complete. But she pulls me, and I itch to delve back into her letters, to pore over the purple inked script that became, over time, more flamboyant and difficult to decipher.

Today I discovered a small envelope with a bold black seal and her words, 'This contains a charm for the journey. F. A. Sept. 1935.' I carefully lift out a mauve card with two dried sprigs of a flower I can't identify, stitched to the card with still-crimson embroidery silk. She has written a message for me to discover nearly 90 years later: 'Smooth seas, speedy transit, fair winds', and she has tucked in a skein of red silk for protection. This is a charm for me, for the journey I'm still on with her.

Fiona Lindsay Shen earned her PhD in Art History from the University of St. Andrews, Scotland, and has worked as an art historian and curator in the United Kingdom, mainland China and the US. She is currently Director of the Escalette Permanent Collection of Art at Chapman University in California. While living in Shanghai, she was associate professor at the Sino-British College from September 2009 to August 2014 and Honorary Editor of the Royal Asiatic Society China Journal from November 2011 to December 2013. She has published in the fields of design and museum studies in Europe and the US, and in 2012 published the monograph Knowledge is Pleasure: Florence Ayscough in Shanghai. *Her recent books are* Silver *(Reaktion Books, 2017) and* Pearl: Nature's Perfect Gem *(Reaktion Books, 2022).*

REFERENCES

1. Lindsay Shen, *Knowledge is Pleasure: Florence Ayscough in Shanghai* (Hong Kong: Hong Kong University Press, RAS China series, 2012).
2. Herbert A. Giles, letter to Florence Ayscough, 9 December, 1925. Harley MacNair Papers, Special Collections, Armacost Library, University of Redlands.
3. Reginald Fleming Johnston, letter to Florence Ayscough, 3 June, 1915, Harley MacNair Papers, Armacost Library.
4. Z. J. Woo, letter to Florence Ayscough, 18 December, 1926. Harley MacNair Papers, Armacost Library.
5. Florence Wheelock Ayscough and Amy Lowell, *Florence Ayscough & Amy Lowell: Correspondence of a Friendship* (Chicago: University of Chicago Press, 1945).
6. Francis [sic] Ayscough, 'Phantasmagoria,' *Ostasiatische Zeitschrift* vol. 5, 1929, pp. 46-8.
7. Florence Ayscough, handwritten annotations on offprint of 'Phantasmagoria,' Harley MacNair Papers, Armacost Library.

IN THE FOOTSTEPS OF COL JAMES TOD:
A BICENTENARY TOUR OF RAJASTHAN
By Dr Elizabeth Driver

ABSTRACT

In this, its bicentenary year, the Royal Asiatic Society (RAS) is celebrating the life and work of Lt Col James Tod, the first Political Agent appointed by the East India Company in Rajasthan in the early years of the 19th century; author of the Annals and Antiquities of Rajasthan *and a founding member of the RAS. In 2023, a group from the RAS followed in his footsteps, using his writings to guide their way.*

INTRODUCTION

Lt-Col James Tod was the first Political Agent to be appointed by the East India Company in Rajasthan in the early years of the 19th century. He is the author of the *Annals and Antiquities of Rajasthan*[1], published originally in two volumes in 1829 and 1832 respectively, and republished with a third volume of additional material prepared by Norbert Peabody. The *Annals* cover many aspects of Rajasthan, including geography, topography, agriculture, ethnography and, perhaps most importantly, the history, mythology and genealogy of the Rajput ruling families. Tod created a master list of the Thirty-Six Royal Races, of whom the Sisodias of Mewar, descended from the Sun God, were pre-eminent. He constantly seeks to draw parallels between the heroic Rajputs and the Greek and Roman heroes, thus legitimising the Rajputs to European readers.

In India, the *Annals* are still read and, as Freitag[2] suggests, in Rajasthan, Tod is still the 'marker and preserver of the bygone glory of the Rajputs'. Until recently, Indian school children read Tod and a copy of the *Annals* is apparently still a common wedding present in Rajasthan.

Tod was also the first librarian of the Royal Asiatic Society so, in this, our bicentenary year, it seemed appropriate to follow in his footsteps to some of the well-known and more obscure parts of Rajasthan. Tod described the three journeys he made over a short period as Political Agent from 1818 to 1822 in the Personal Narrative sections of the *Annals*. Based on this, I made two visits, in October

2022 and with a group in February 2023.

To understand how he, a British officer, became so important in Rajasthan we must first look at the state of Rajasthan when Tod arrived in 1799.

RAJASTHAN AT THE BEGINNING OF THE 19TH CENTURY: MARATHAS AND PINDARIS

The Marathas had been raiding north-west India, into Malwa and Gujarat, throughout the 18th century and the decline in Mughal power to check them had led to incursions into neighbouring Rajasthan. They invaded Mewar in 1711 and attacked Bundi and Kotah in 1726. They became involved in Rajput internecine disputes, mainly over succession, at the invitation of the Rajputs themselves, who ended up promising to pay them enormous sums of money, which they then couldn't pay, resulting in territory being ceded.

The Marathas were assisted by the Pindaris, 'irregular troops attached to the Maratha armies, used mainly for plunder'. Tod often used the term 'freebooter' to describe them. One of their leaders, Amir Khan, had assisted the Marathas, but then skilfully exploited differences between the Rajput rulers, supporting whoever seemed expedient at the time. At the end of the Pindari war in 1818, the British bought him off by making him Nawab of Tonk, where he continued to cause trouble.

The end result of all this was that the land was laid waste, villages burnt, trade and commerce made impossible and there was a massive migration of population out of Rajasthan.

As the British expansion came up against Maratha ambitions, three Anglo-Maratha wars were fought between the East India Company and the Maratha Empire. The third Anglo-Maratha War (1817-1819) resulted in the break-up of the Maratha empire and, under the Treaty of Gwalior, Scindia surrendered Rajasthan to the British and agreed to help them fight the Pindaris. Tod's map and local intelligence had proved a crucial strategic tool in this war. Tod was attached to the court of Scindia as the commander of the British escort, effectively to keep an eye on him.

The Rajputs realised that the British would protect them from the Marathas and between 1803 and 1823, all the Rajput states signed treaties with the East India Company (EIC). The EIC agreed not to interfere in internal matters of state, a promise which was broken almost as soon as the treaties had been signed.

Another major contributing factor to the poor state of Rajasthan was the widespread strife between the putative rulers and the local nobles. In Mewar, the treaty with the EIC included an understanding, the Kaul-Nama, between the local nobles and Bhim Singh. The rush to sign it was led by the chief of Begu.

In addition, Jaipur, Jodhpur and Udaipur were engaged in what is sometimes known as the Ten Year War, ostensibly over the hand of the daughter of Bhim Singh of Udaipur, the, of course, beautiful and tragic Krishna Kunwari. Tod tells us:

> Krishna Kunwari (the virgin Krishna) was the name of the lovely object, the rivalry for whose hand assembled under the banners of her suitors (Jagat Singh of Jaipur and Man Singh of Marwar), not only their native chivalry, but all the predatory powers of India; and who, like Helen of old, involved in destruction her own and rival houses.

The situation escalated in part due to the involvement of the ubiquitous and perfidious Pindari, Amir Khan, who initially supported Jaipur and besieged Jodhpur, but then switched sides and was dispatched in 1810 by Man Singh to Udaipur to 'persuade' Bhim Singh that his daughter should marry Man Singh. The story ended badly when her father was advised that the only way out of the impasse was the death of the princess. Her uncle is said to have administered poison, which she took willingly to save her family and land; it was only with the third cup that she died.

Tod's Role
When we first meet him on his travels, at Bamolia in 1807, Tod was Commander of the British escort to the court of Scindia. The court was peripatetic, which gave Tod the opportunity to explore, record and map large parts of Rajasthan. Scindia had already signed a treaty with the EIC and Tod was involved in the negotiation and implementation of further treaties with Rajput rulers.

Tod was then appointed, and dismissed, as Political Agent as follows:

States	Appointed	Dismissed
Western Rajput States: Mewar, Kota, Bundi, Sirohi	1818	All except Mewar by April 1822 Resigned from Mewar June 1822
Marwar	1819	November 1819, at the request of the Jodhpur court
Jaiselmer	1821	1822

Figure 1: Tod's appointments as a Political Agent

Freitag[3] points out that Tod's work as political agent was unique in that he approached it as a historian, on one occasion describing 400 years of history as background to a report on an 1818 border dispute in Sirohi. There is no question that he was fascinated by the Rajputs and sought a link between their martial characteristics and his own Scottish ancestors. He formed close relationships with some, particularly in Udaipur and in Bundi.

It should not be forgotten that he was a product of the Romantic era: Wordsworth, Keats, Shelley, Robert Burns and Walter Scott were contemporaries. Antiquarianism was all the rage. The Rajput construct of valour, chivalry and sacrifice appealed to Tod and he identified with them and tended to ignore their less admirable qualities.

UDAIPUR

Tod first visited Udaipur with Scindia in 1806 when an attempt was made to end the conflict between Mewar and the Marathas. Tod was struck by the romantic appeal of the Rana, Bhim Singh, and wrote in the *Annals*:

> The impression made on the author upon this occasion by the miseries and the noble appearance of this 'descendant of a hundred kings' was never allowed to weaken, but kindled an enthusiastic desire for the restoration of his fallen condition, which stimulated his perseverance to obtain that knowledge by which alone he [Tod] might be enabled to benefit him.

He got his chance twelve years later when he returned to Udaipur as Political Agent. By this time, the situation was even worse: a civil war between two rival Rajput factions had rendered the court unable to function and the nobles had usurped much of the crown lands and were extorting money from the Rana. Because the British were primarily interested in Mewar as a bulwark against the Marathas and as a source of revenue, Tod was instructed by Hastings to 're-establish the Rana's authority and settle the country'.

HOUSE OF RAMPYARI—NOW BOHEDA KI HAVELI

Tod's success in restoring the Rana's position, lands and revenues unsurprisingly made him something of a hero to Bhim Singh, considered a weak ruler, much under the influence of his mother and her friend Rampyari. The previous Maharana was still a minor when he succeeded and his mother assumed the role of regent; it was she who raised the intelligent and ingenious Rampyari to the role of de facto ruler of Mewar. Bhim Singh, was also a minor and the same arrangement continued, even into his majority. It was in Rampyari's orchards, now long since built on, that Tod set up his camp and lived for three years.

TOD LEAVES UDAIPUR ON HIS FIRST JOURNEY

Tod set out from Udaipur on the first of his journeys on 11 October 1819. He was clearly well settled in:

> We had our palace in the city, our cutter on the lake, our villa in the woods, our fairy islands in the waters; streams to angle in, deer to shoot, much, in short, to please the eye and gratify the taste:- yet did ennui intrude, and all panted to escape from the 'happy valley' to see what was in the world beyond the mountains.

It was quite an entourage: Tod, his cousin Captain Patrick Waugh, Waugh's ensign, Lt Carey, and Doctor Duncan and also the man Tod describes as his guru, a Jain called Gyanachandra, on whom he was dependent for translation and interpretation. They were accompanied by two companies of foot and sixty of Skinner's Horse, the 'yellow boys'.

TOD'S HOUSE

They set off at 5am and reached camp by 8.

> The spot chosen, and where I afterwards built a residence, was a rising ground between the villages of Merta and Toos, sprinkled with trees and, for a space of four miles, clear of the belt of forest which fringes the granite barriers of the valley [...] to the south, a mile distant, we had the Berach river, abounding in trout; and the noble lake whence it issues, called after its founder, the Udai Sagar, was not more than three to the west.

Figure 2a: Tod's house at Dabok, Udaipur in 1893

Figure 2b: Tod's house in 2023

He refers to it again on his return from his first journey, when he had to wait at Merta for a few days to be formally welcomed back to Udaipur by Bhim Singh. 'Here we amused ourselves in chalking out the site of our projected residence on the heights of Tus, and in fishing in the source of the Berach'.

The building that we located in 2022 is between Merta and Toos, at Dabok. It is now a Teacher Training College and we were welcomed, with ceremony, in 2023 by its Principal, Professor Saroj Garg, and her staff. I am convinced that the building we visited is the same as that seen in ruins in a photograph taken in 1893.

We will return to Tod's house, and the final poignant reference to it, right at the end of his Personal Narratives.

Ahar

Like Tod, we visited the royal cenotaphs at Ahar. 'Ar or Ahar, near where we encamped, is sacred to the manes of the Princes of Udaipur, and contains the cenotaphs of all her kings since the valley became their residence; but as they do not disdain association, either in life or death, with their vassal, Ar presents the appearance of a thickly crowded cemetery...'

Figure 3: The royal cenotaphs at Ahar

Figure 4: Bhim Singh rides out to welcome Tod to Udaipur

GREETING BY MAHARANA BHIM SINGH ON TOD'S RETURN TO UDAIPUR.
At last, the signs were auspicious and Bhim Singh rode out to welcome Tod back. I think this passage shows well the closeness of the relationship between the Maharana and Tod: 'The Rana came, attended by his son, his chief minister, and, in fact, all the capital in his train. The most hearty welcomes were lavished upon us all […] it was not a meeting of formality, but of well-cemented friendship'.

AN AGRICULTURAL INTERLUDE: OPIUM CULTURE
The agricultural practices of Rajasthan clearly fascinated Tod and he tells us a good deal about what crops were grown at the various times of the year. What is most interesting is what he has to say about opium:

> A slight sketch of the introduction and mode of culture of this drug, which has tended more to the physical and moral degradation of the inhabitants than the combined influence of pestilence and war, may not be without interest.

He suggests that medicinal use dates back to antiquity but that abuse is relatively recent, or not more than three centuries back. He goes on to describe the method of cultivation and harvest:

> The cutting instrument consists of three prongs[…] The wound is made from the base up and the milky juice which exudes coagulates on the outside. Each plant is

thrice pierced on three successive days, the operation commencing as soon as the sun begins to warm. In cold mornings, when it congeals rapidly, the coagulation is taken off with a scraper.

The method remains unchanged.

Figure 5a and 5b: Opium cultivation

Tod is damning about the British exploitation of opium:

> If the now paramount power, instead of making a monopoly of it, and consequently extending the cultivation, would endeavour to restrict it by judicious legislative enactments, or at least reduce its culture to what it was forty years ago, generations yet unborn would have just reason to praise us for this work of mercy. It is no less our interest than our duty to do so, and to call forth genuine industry, for the improvement of cotton, indigo, sugar-cane, and other products which would enrich instead of demoralising, and therefore impoverishing, the country. We have saved Rajputana from political ruin; but the boon of mere existence will be valueless if we fail to restore the moral energies of her population

SOME COUNTRY FORTS AND RAJPUT HOSPITALITY

We visited some smaller forts in the countryside where we were lavishly entertained by the descendants of the rulers with whom Tod worked.

Strictly speaking, Bamolia should not have been part of this tour, which was otherwise based on the Personal Narrative sections of the *Annals*, as Tod visited in 1807, as a young man. However, it is associated with such a funny incident and so well illustrates what Tod was doing in the earlier part of his career that a visit was irresistible, and Maharaj Abhimanyu Singh Bambulia gave us a very warm welcome. Tod describes his visit:

> In 1807, when the author, then commencing his career, was wandering alone through their country, surveying their geography, and collecting scraps of their statistics, he left Scindia battering Rathgurh, and was returning home unattended at a brisk canter, when, as he passed through the town of Bamolia, a party rushed out and made him captive, saying that he must visit the chief. Although much fatigued, it would have been folly to refuse. He obeyed, and was conveyed to a square, in the centre of which was an elevated chabootra or platform, shaded by the sacred tree. Here, sitting on carpets, was the chief with his little court. The Author was received most courteously. The first act was to disembarrass him of his boots; but this, heated as he was, they could not effect: refreshments were then put before him, and a Brahmin brought water, with a ewer and basin for his ablutions. Although he was then but an indifferent linguist, and their patois scarcely intelligible to him, he passed a very happy hour, in which conversation never flagged.

BANERA: THE LOST PISTOLS

Tod described Banera when he visited it in early December 1820 as '… one of the most imposing feudal edifices of Mewar, and its lord one of the greatest of its chieftains'. He goes on to explain how it was only by chance that one of two sons born to Rana Raj on the same day but of different wives became the ruler of Mewar at Udaipur and the other the chief of Banera. Consequently, even today, on the succession to the gaddi of a new Raja of Banera, the Maharana of Mewar sends the ceremonial sword to Banera, unlike the other Mewari nobles who have to go to Udaipur for formal investiture. The new Raja then goes to Udaipur and the Maharana honours him by receiving him at the city gate.

Tod said of his meeting with Raja Bhim: 'I had a good opportunity of observing the feudal state and manners of these chiefs within their own domains during a visit of three hours at Banera'.

The description of the conversation with Raja Bhim gives some insight into how Tod operated. 'The 'velvet cushion' was spread in a balcony projecting from the main hall of Banera'. The Raja asked Tod's advice as his 'adopted brother' on matters of domestic and rural economy, a dispute over a marriage settlement, bad relations between the Raja and his vassals.

> All these arbitrations were made without reference to my official situation, but were forced upon me merely by the claims of friendship; but it was a matter of exultation that enabled me to make use of my influence for the adjustment of such disputes, and for restoring individual as well as general prosperity

Rana Bhim presented Tod with gifts then 'My friend accompanied me to my tents, when I presented to him a pair of pistols...' Unfortunately, the pistols have recently been stolen. It transpired that all old arms had had to be surrendered to the police and that the pistols had been in the armoury of the police station in Bhilwara. They were last seen in 2021 and have since disappeared.

Begu: A Visit to Not See a Gateway

We had to go to Begu because it was the scene of one of the most dramatic incidents in the *Annals*, which occurred in February 1822, described by Tod with charming, and unusual, self-deprecation.

> The chances were nine hundred and ninety-nine to one that I ever touched a pen again. Two days ago, I started, with all the 'pomp and circumstance' befitting the occasion, to restore to the chief the land of his sires, of which force and fraud had conspired to deprive them during more than thirty years. The old castle of Begun has a remarkably wide moat, across which there is a wooden bridge communicating with the town.

The rest of Tod's party had crossed the bridge and entered the castle. The mahout told Tod that there would not be space to admit Tod's elephant and howdah through the gate.

> But I heedlessly told him to drive on, and if he could not pass through, to dismount. The hollow sound of the bridge, and the deep moat on either side, alarmed the animal, and she darted forward with the celerity occasioned by fear, in spite of any effort to stop her. As I approached the gateway, I measured it with my eye, and expecting inevitable and instantaneous destruction, I planted my feet firmly against the howda, and my forearms against the archway, and, by an almost preternatural effort of strength, burst out of the back of the howda; the elephant pursued her flight inside, and I dropped senseless to the bridge below.

Tod was taken to his camp and put to bed. The Rawat ordered that the gate be demolished, saying 'he could never have looked on it with complacency, since it had nearly deprived of life one who had given life to them'. This was a reference to the fact that the Marathas under Scindia had taken over Begu and were exacting a heavy payment. This was brought to an end by the treaty with the EIC, which Begu was the first to sign.

Two Important Rajput Forts
Tod was greatly moved by the great Rajput forts of Kumbalgarh and Chittorgarh, which he visited under very different circumstances.

Kumbalgarh
Kumbalgarh had been the site of one of his major diplomatic triumphs and his reception by the Maharaja Daulat Singh in 1820 was correspondingly effusive. In February 1818, Kumbalgarh was occupied by a Maratha garrison. Luckily for Tod, they were mercenaries who had not been paid and he was able to negotiate with them for possession on payment of the arrears. He didn't have anything like enough cash on him but he provided a bill of exchange.

> Next morning, we saw them winding down the western declivity, while we quietly took our breakfast in an old

ruined temple. My own escort remained in possession for a week, until the Rana sent his garrison. During these eight days our time was amply occupied in sketching and deciphering the monumental records of this singularly diversified spot.

Tod found much to admire and drew parallels with various forms of classical architecture. He described the battlements as having 'a strong resemblance to the Etruscan'. There are over 300 temples within the fort wall, most of them Jain. Waugh's drawing of the Parsvanath Jain temple shows what Tod means when he extols its classicism.

The design of this temple is truly classic. [...] The architecture is undoubtedly Jain, which is as distinct from the Brahmanical as their religion [...] There is a chasteness and simplicity in this specimen of monotheistic worship, affording a wide contrast to the elaborately sculpted shrines of the Saivas, and other polytheists of India.

He considers that the extreme want of decoration shows that it is ancient, dating to the time of Chandragupta, two hundred years before Christ. He speculates on the relationship between Chandragupta and the Greeks and tells us that the daughter of the Rajput king was married to Seleucus. 'It is curious to contemplate the possibility, nay the probability, that the Jain temple now before the reader may have

Figure 6: Waugh's drawing of the Parsvanath Jain temple

been designed by Grecian artists, or that the taste of the Rajputs may have been modelled after the Grecian. This was our temple of Theseus in Mewar'.

He rather destroys his own argument by telling us about another Jain temple in the vicinity consisting of three storeys '...offering a perfect contrast to that described'. Many of the others have elaborate carvings

Tod's party found some difficulty in descending from Kumbalgarh to the north. 'Rumour had not magnified the difficulties of the descent, which we found strewed with our baggage, arresting all progress for a full hour'. But they enjoyed the fresh mountain air and the magnificent mountain scenery. Carey had an accident:

> There was one spot where the waters formed a pool. Little Carey was determined to trust his pony to carry him across, but deviating to the left, just as I was leaping from a projecting ledge, to my horror, horse and rider disappeared. The shock was momentary, and a good ducking the only result, which in the end was the luckiest thing that could have befallen him.

CHITTORGARH

Tod visited Chittorgarh, or Chittor, as a tourist on his return from his final visit to Bundi for the investiture of the new, child, ruler. By then he was very ill and had just been badly injured at Begun so he was being carried in a palki. Nonetheless, he tells us he reserved the little strength he had for Chittor. He ascended the steep road through the five great gates on the same elephant he had been riding at Begu; 'in passing under each successive portal, I felt an involuntary tendency to stoop, though there was a superfluity of room overhead'. It was worth it:

> My heart beat high as I approached the ancient capital of the Sesodias, teeming with reminiscences of glory, which every stone in her giant-like battlements attested.

He describes the ruins in great detail, particularly the Pillar of Victory erected by Rana Kumbh on his defeat of the combined armies of Malwa and Gujarat in 1440. 'It is one mass of sculpture; of which a better idea cannot be conveyed than in the remark of those who dwell about it, that it contains every object known to their mythology'.

Below the site of the Tower is the '...scene of the awful Johar, on the occasion of Ala sacking Chittor when the Queens perished in the flames'. Ala was Allauddin Khalji, the Sultan of Delhi, and it was he who, having besieged the fort in 1303, was said to have told Rana Ratan Singh that he would spare the city if he could meet Padmini, the beautiful Queen. Of course, it is a tale of betrayal and tragedy. Chittor was won back from the Khaljis but finally fell to Akbar in 1567. Unfortunately, the romantic story is likely a myth and certainly the palace of Padmini we saw long postdates the events; Giles Tillotson[4] says that the present building is a 19th century replica of an earlier 16th century palace.

Tod spent three days exploring the ruins. 'I gazed until the sun's last rays fell upon the "ringlet of Chittor", illuminating its grey and grief-worn aspect, like a lambent gleam lighting up the face of sorrow'.

SOME TEMPLES
BAROLLI

Tod visited the temples at Barolli, which are now known to date from the 9th and 10th centuries, and were, as Tod described them, in a remarkable state of preservation in November 1821. By this time, all his compatriots were seriously ill or, in the case of Carey, dead.

> Art seems here to have exhausted itself, and we were, perhaps for the first time, fully impressed with the beauty of Hindu sculpture. The columns, the ceilings, the external roofing, where each stone presents a miniature temple, one rising over another, until crowned by the urn like kalas...

I can't help thinking that Tod's belated admiration for Hindu architecture might have had something to do with the columns, which were recorded exquisitely in the contemporary drawings and might be regarded as resembling the classical European architecture so admired by Tod and his contemporaries. He describes them as 'excelling everything yet described'.

To give him credit, Tod was also moved by the Hindu sculptures in the niches on the exterior of the main temple and by a fragmented Ganesha. The temples are still astonishing and thriving. An orange

Figure 7b:
Baroli, 2023

Figure 7a: Waugh's drawing of the 'classical' columns at Barolli

Hanuman is provided with sandals of various sizes in case he wants to go for a walk in the woods.

MENAL

Tod's party visited Menal a couple of days later. He enthuses, not for the first or last time, that 'It is fortunate that the pencil can here portray what transcends the power of the pen'. The site of the Menal temples is spectacular and unusual.

> It is difficult to conceive what could have induced the princely races of Chitor and Ajmer to select such a spot […] which in summer must be a furnace, owing to the reflection of the sun's rays from the rock; tradition, indeed, asserts that it is to the love of the sublime alone we are indebted for these singular structures.

Tod describes the setting of the two groups of temples on either side of a great chasm. He imagined the 'last two bulwarks of the Rajput races' meeting, with their families, before all were killed fighting the Muslim invaders at Chittor. It was *'pralaya'*, the day of universal doom of the poets.

> To me, who have pored over their poetic legends, and imbibed all those sympathies which none can avoid who study the Rajput character, there was a melancholy charm in the solemn ruins of Menal. It was a season, too, when

everything conspired to nourish this feeling; the very trees which were crowded about these relics of departed glory, appearing by their leafless boughs and lugubrious aspect to join the universal mourning.

BIJOLIA

Bijolia was part of the Mewar kingdom and was developed during the Chauhan dynasty, 7th to 12th century, when it was known as Morakara. Several inscriptions, translated for Tod by Gyanachandra, confirm the history of the site and are still visible. Tod refers to the modern castle of Bijolia being constructed out of the ruins of Morakara. There were many carved stones in the walls of the present fort and the gateways of the fort and of the palace were clearly constructed from old temple carvings. Tod tells us:

> This is very common, as we have repeatedly noticed; nor can anything better evince that the Hindu attaches no abstract virtue to the material objector idol, but regards it merely as a type of some power or quality which he wishes to propitiate. On the desecration of the receptacle, the idol becomes again, in his estimation, a mere stone, and is used as such without scruple.

I am not sure that Christians are any different. I have seen many farm houses built with the stones of abbeys.

KOTAH

In the Personal Narrative, Tod describes his arrival in Kotah in February 1820, promising us that he will have more to say about the city during their halt, 'which is likely to be of some continuance'. In fact, he had nothing to say until they left four months later when he explains:

> The last four months [...] was a continued struggle against cholera and deadly fever; never in the memory of man was such a season known. This is not a state of mind or body fit for recording passing events; and although the period of the last six months... has been one of the most eventful of my life, it has left fewer traces of these events

on my mind for notice in my journal than if I had been less occupied.

He tells us how they changed the site of their camp several times in an attempt to escape the heat and sickness, to no avail: 'Scarcely any place can be more unhealthy than Kota during the monsoon'.

ZALIM SINGH

Tantalisingly, Tod tells us of his parting from the Maharao and his brothers and from the Regent, Zalim Singh.

> The man who had passed through such scenes as the reader has perused, now at the very verge of existence, could not repress his sorrow. His orbless eyes were filled with tears, and as I pressed his palsied hands which were extended over me, the power of utterance entirely deserted him. I would expunge this if I did not know that vanity has no share in what I consider to be a virtue in the regent. I have endeavoured to paint his character, and could not omit this trait. I felt he had a regard for me, from a multitude of kind expressions, but of their full value was always doubtful to this day.

To find out what this refers to, we have to turn to the history of Kotah which Tod wrote up, with the benefit of hindsight, for the *Annals* after his return to England. Of one hundred pages, ninety are mostly devoted to Zalim Singh. Zalim Singh was a very old man by the time Tod visited in 1820, having been born in 1739 into a family of hereditary Faujdars of Kotah—meaning governor and military commander, so a position of great power. As a young man Zalim Singh had twice saved Kotah from defeat, first from Jaipur in 1761 at the battle of Mangrol, and then from Holkar, one of the Maratha rulers, whose help he had earlier enlisted to defeat Jaipur.

When the ten year old Umaid Singh came to the throne in 1771, Zalim Singh became the Regent, increasing his power, effectively becoming the ruler of Kotah throughout Umaid Singh's nominal reign. He disposed of all opposition, reorganised the army, reformed land tax, negotiated with the Marathas and Pindaris, even providing them with a fort and land in order to keep Kotah safe from them. Tod tells us how Zalim Singh operated:

> His lynx-like eye saw at once who was likely to invade his authority, and these knew their peril from the vigilance of a system which never relaxed. Entire self-reliance, a police such as perhaps no country in the world could equal, establishments well paid, services liberally rewarded, character and talent in each department of the State, himself keeping a strict watch overall, and trusting implicitly to none, with a daily personal supervision of all this complicated state-machinery—such was the system which surmounted every peril, and not only maintained but increased the power and political reputation of Zalim Singh, amidst the storms of war, rapine, treason, and political convulsions for more than a century.

In December 1817, Kotah entered into a treaty of subsidiary alliance with the East India Company, the treaty being signed by Maharao Umaid Singh. In the initial treaty, no power was vested in the Regent, who is only mentioned in the preamble. Tod explains that in March 1818, two supplemental articles were agreed, guaranteeing the administration of the State to Zalim Singh and to his sons and successors for ever. Tod comments:

> There is not a shadow of doubt that the supplemental articles of the treaty of Kotah, which pledged our faith to two parties in a manner which rendered its maintenance towards both an impossibility, produced consequences that shook the confidence of the people of Rajwara in our political rectitude.

The issue came to a head when Umaid Singh died and his successor challenged Zalim Singh's dominance over the state. This civil war culminated in another battle at Mangrol, in 1821, at which the British supported Zalim Singh but Tod was perceived by his superiors to have supported the Maharao, who was defeated. Tod was dismissed as Political Agent to Kotah.

TOD'S BRIDGE

After the signing of the Treaty, the East India Company and the Kotah army under Zalim Singh joined forces to defeat the Pindaris. The plunder taken was used to fund the building of a bridge over a tributary of the Chambal river which was dedicated to Marquis Hastings, the Governor General of British India. It appears that Zalim Singh, perhaps embarrassed by his role in defeating his erstwhile allies, handed over all the plunder to Tod.

TOD'S HORSE

Tod was presented with a splendid horse called Baj-raj by Rana Bhim Singh. This horse died and was buried in Kotah.

> Baj-raj [...] was perfection, and so general a favourite, that his death was deemed a public misfortune [...] The general yell of sorrow that burst from all my sepoys and establishment on that event, was astounding, and the whole camp attended his obsequies; many were weeping, and when they began to throw the earth upon the fine beast, wrapped in his body clothes, his groom threw himself into his grave, and was quite frantic with grief. I cut some locks off his mane in remembrance of the noblest beast I ever crossed, and in a few days I observed many huge stones near the spot, which before I left Kotah grew into a noble altar of hewn stone about twenty feet square and four feet high, on which was placed the effigy of Baj-raj large as life, sculpted out of one block of freestone.

Astonishingly the statue of the horse is still there, at the side of a dual carriageway and overshadowed by one of the great roundabouts which are being built all over Kotah.

BUNDI: TOD'S FIRST VISIT

Still very unwell, Tod travelled from Kota to Bundi in September 1820 and was greeted by the Raja. This would have been Bishen Singh, who had assisted the East India Company in their fight against Holkar. The Marathas and the Pindaris had plundered and invaded Bundi incessantly with both Holkar and Scindia taking over land and exacting a large tribute. In 1818, Bundi signed a treaty with the East

India Company and Tod was appointed Political Agent.

Tod was on an elephant when the Raja appeared on horseback so he rapidly dismounted and mounted his own horse, Javadia. Unfortunately, Javadia's 'warlike propensities' were awakened and he started to show off. 'In one of his furious bounds, he had his feet on the parapet of a reservoir, and as I turned him short, he threw up his head, which came into contact with mine [...] and a few more bounds brought me in contact with my friend the Rao Raja'. Tod describes the Bundi palace:

> The coup d'oeil of the castellated palace of Bundi, from whichever side you approach it, is perhaps the most striking in India; but it would require a drawing on a much larger scale to comprehend either its picturesque beauties or its grandeur [...]. It is an aggregate of palaces, each having the name of its founder; and yet the whole so well harmonises, and the character of the architecture is so uniform, that its breaks or fantasies appear to arise only from the peculiarity of the position, and serve to diversify its beauties.
>
> Gardens are intermingled with palaces raised on gigantic terraces. In one of these, I was received by the Raja the next day. Whoever has seen the palace of Bundi, can easily picture to himself the hanging gardens of Semiramis.

They stayed a week because first Dr Duncan and then Lt Carey were so ill and Tod himself was still in bed. 'Our friend the doctor, who has been ailing for some time, grew gradually worse, and at length gave himself up. Carey found him destroying his papers and making his will, and came over deeply affected. No sooner than he was a little mended than Carey took to his bed'. They departed, all in litters, and reached Udaipur at the end of October. Carey died when they were almost back and was buried at Merta.

BUNDI: TOD'S SECOND VISIT

The Rao Raja had made Tod guardian of his young heir and in July 1821 he received the news that the Rao Raja had died of cholera and a summons to return to Bundi, where palace intrigues were threatening the stability of the court and the life of the child heir. They reached

Bundi at the end of July, in torrential rain.

Tod describes the ceremony of Rajtilak, or investiture, of the eleven year old Prince Ram Singh. The ceremony took place in the Rajmahall, with crowds of cheering people assembled in the courtyard below.

> The young prince went through a number of propitiatory rites with singular accuracy and self-possession; and when they were over, the assembly rose. I was then requested to conduct him to the gaddi, placed in an elevated balcony overlooking the external court. It being too high for the young prince to reach, I raised him to it.

A priest brought an unction of sandalwood paste and aromatic oils and 'I dipped the middle finger of my right hand and made the tilak on his forehead'.

Figure 8: The gaddi in the Palace of Bundi on which
Tod conducted the Rajtilak ceremony

CENOTAPHS AND SATI

Tod refers to the cenotaphs at Bundi in the context of sati. These cenotaphs are particularly atmospheric and beautifully carved, situated beside a lake, probably near to where Tod camped. Tod is horrified by the sixty four females who committed sati when Ajit Singh of Jodhpur died, but comments that it is twenty less than when his contemporary, Budh Singh of Bundi, was drowned.

The monuments of this noble family of the Haras are far more explicit than those of the Rathors, for every such sati is sculpted on a small altar in the centre of the cenotaph: which speaks in distinct language the all-powerful motive, vanity, the principal incentive to these tremendous sacrifices.

He is clearly proud that the last command of his friend the Rao Raja of Bundi was to prohibit his wives from committing sati. Tod tells us that his command was religiously obeyed.

JODHPUR AND MAN SINGH

Tod visited Jodhpur on his first journey from Udaipur in early November 1819, the year in which he was appointed Political Agent to Marwar. The Raja was Man Singh. Tod tells us, writing with hindsight:

The biography of Man Singh would afford a remarkable picture of human patience, fortitude, and constancy, never surpassed in any age or country. But in this school of adversity, he also took lessons in cruelty: he learned therein to master or rather disguise his passions; and though he showed not the ferocity of the tiger, he acquired the still more dangerous attribute of that animal- its cunning. At that very time, not long after he had emerged from his seclusion, while his features were modelled into an expression of complaisant self-content, indicative of a disdain for human greatness, he was weaving his web of destruction for numberless victims who were basking in the sunshine of his favour.

This requires some explanation. Man Singh's predecessor was Bhim Singh. He had come to power in 1792 with the help of the Thakur of Pokhran and promptly set about eliminating all his potential rivals until only his cousin, Man Singh survived and he had fled to the fort of Jalore. Bhim Singh sent several expeditions but each failed to take the fort and when Bhim Singh died in 1803, Man Singh, was held to be the heir to the throne. The siege of Jalore was lifted and Man Singh was invested in January 1804. His old enemy, the Thakur of Pokhran, claimed that the rightful heir was a posthumous son born to one of

Bhim Singh's wives. A significant number of other rulers backed this claim and Man Singh was besieged again, this time in Jodhpur fort.

As so often, a major player in all this was the wily Pindari chief, Amir Khan, who changed sides at will. Having decided to support Man Singh, he tricked his enemies, including Pokhran, into accepting an invitation to a reception. They were murdered in a massive tent erected for the purpose. Man Singh later sent Amir Singh to Udaipur to demand Krishna Kumari in marriage, with tragic consequences.

Predictably, Amir Khan changed sides again and, this time in league with Man Singh's son, Chhatar Singh, and his mother, assassinated Man Singh's trusted finance minister and his Nath guru. Man Singh was persuaded to hand over the administration of the state to his son as Regent. He went into seclusion and is said to have become insane. It was Chhatar Singh who signed the treaty with the East India Company in January 1818 but he died two months later. Man Singh resumed the administration of Marwar. He set about executing those whom he held responsible for the murders of his advisors, plus many more Marwari nobles. Others fled. This was the situation when Tod arrived.

Astonishingly, Tod seems to have ignored most of this and sympathised with Man Singh. They met formally on several occasions and also had a lengthy private meeting of which Tod says:

> I received the most convincing proofs of his intelligence, and minute knowledge of past history [...] he was remarkably well-read; and at this and other visits, he afforded me much instruction. He had copies made for me of the chief histories of his family, which are now deposited in the library of the Royal Asiatic Society. He entered deeply into the events of his personal history, and recounted many expedients he was obliged to have recourse to in order to save his life, when, in consequence of the murder of his Guru [...] he relinquished the reins of power and acquiesced in their assumption by his son.
>
> I went to take leave of the Raja. I left him in the full expectation that his energy of character would surmount the difficulties with which he was surrounded, though not without a struggle...
>
> With mutual good wishes, and a request for literary

correspondence, which was commenced but soon closed, I bade adieu to Raja Man and the capital of Marwar.

But, in the six months following Tod's visit, Man Singh embarked on a spate of killings:

Each day announced a numerous list of victims, either devoted to death, or imprisoned and stripped of their wealth.

Tod was relieved of his position as Political Agent of Marwar, apparently at the request of the Court.

A DAY OFF IN MANDORE

Following his meetings with Man Singh, Tod had a day off in Mandore, the former capital of Marwar. He admired the cenotaphs, which look more like temples than other cenotaphs seen by Tod or by us. Tod was much taken with the painted stone sculptures of Rajput heroes which he considered had a 'singularly pleasing effect'.

They are cut out of the rock but entirely detached from it, and larger than life […] Each chieftain is armed with lance, sword and buckler […] All are painted; but whether in the colours they were attached to, or according to the fancy of the architect, I know not.

He was particularly taken with Pabuji mounted on Kesar Kali. Had one not known that these statues were created in 1707 in the reign of Ajit Singh, one might have attributed them to an Indian Disney.

Figure 9a: Waugh's drawing of Pabuji mounted on Kesar Kali at Mandore
Figure 9b: Pabuji mounted on Kesar Kali, 2023

After climbing up to the old fort, seeing the other group of cenotaphs and admiring the palace and its gardens, Tod committed an act of vandalism.

> The day was now nearly departed, and it was time for me to return to my friends in camp. I finished the evening by another visit to the knights of the desert; and, inscribing my name on the foot of Black Caesar, bade adieu to the ancient Mandore.

Tod's Farewell to Udaipur

Tod returned to Udaipur for the last time in March 1822 and saw the progress on his house.

> I halted a few days at Mairta, and found my house nearly finished, and the garden looking beautiful [...] some of the finest peaches are the produce of those I planted at Gwalior, I may say their grandchildren. When I left Gwalior in 1817, I brought with me the stones of several peach trees, and planted them in the garden of Rang-Pyari, my residence in Oodipoor; and more delicious or more abundant fruit I never saw. The stones of these I again put in the new garden at Mairta [...] The vegetables were equally thriving [...] the Rana has monopolised the celery, which he pronounces the prince of vegetables. I had also got my cutter for the Udaisagar, and we promised ourselves many delightful days, sailing amidst islets and fishing in its stream.

It was not to be and, right at the end of the *Annals*, Tod writes sadly of the death of Carey and the ill health of Dr Duncan, about to depart for the Cape, and Waugh, left behind at Kotah to try to sort out the chaos. 'I looked on all the works my hands had wrought and on the labour I had laboured to do; and alas, all was vanity and vexation of spirit'. His sadness at having to leave is poignant.

> To all their customs, to all their sympathies, and numerous acts of courtesy and kindness, which have made this not a strange land to me, I am about to bid farewell; whether a

final one is written in that book, which for wise purposes
is sealed to mortal vision: but wherever I go, whatever days
I may number, nor place, nor time can ever waken, far less
obliterate, the remembrance of the valley of Oodipoor.

Saheliyon ki Bari and Farewell to Rana Bhim Singh

Tod retreated to a pavilion and garden lent to him by the Queen of
Bundi, who had made him her brother. Tod's packing and sad farewells
are described at the beginning of his book, Travels in Western India,[5]
published posthumously in 1839.

> A fortnight had been spent in preparations, and in order
> that I might experience less interruption from visitors, I
> retired to the Suhailca-ca bari, a delightful villa belonging
> to the Hara Queen, about a mile north of the capital...

It was here that Tod bade farewell to the Rana:

> The Rana, when he came for the last time to "grant me
> leave", was amused at seeing me surrounded with workmen
> employed in making cases for statues, inscriptions,
> minerals, manuscripts &c. It was a painful interview for
> all parties.

Tod tells how he had transformed the lives of the Rana and his
subjects by subduing 'the predatory Mahratta, the ruthless Pat'han,
the kinsman-foe...' He also makes some rather patronising remarks
about the 'grand secret of European superiority', which seems at odds
with the tone of the Annals. However, the closeness of his relationship
with the Rana is clear:

> On this occasion, instead of his usual good-humoured
> and always instructive loquacity, the Rana was silent and
> thoughtful, and what he did utter was in abrupt sentences,
> with frequent repetitions of "Remember I give you leave
> for only three years" [...] He has served me five years,
> raised the country from ruin, and does not take even a
> pinch of the soil of Mewar with him.

An odd remark given the scale of the packing. There were 40 packing cases in all, the contents of which mostly ended up at the Royal Asiatic Society or in the British Library. On 1 June 1822, Tod left Udaipur for the last time.

THE RECKONING

It is undoubtedly the case that Tod is still seen by many Rajputs as the man who restored their fortunes and brought them to the attention of the western world as a brave and noble race on a par with European heroes such as the Greeks or the Scythians—or Tod's own Scottish ancestors. His achievements are not in doubt, nor is his love for the Rajputs and theirs for him.

Tod's sadness at leaving Rajasthan comes over clearly in the Personal Narratives and in the introduction to his subsequent book, *Travels in Western India*. He clearly intended to stay on in Mewar and left the house and garden he had lavished such attention on unfinished.

Tod's career as Political Agent in Rajasthan was a short one. Much has been written about why and it is clear that the reasons are complex, but it is also clear that Tod did not have the backing of his immediate superior, the Resident in Rajasthan, David Ochterlony. Tod was not good at keeping Ochterlony informed about what he was doing[6] and made his own judgements about who to support. He was sympathetic to the weak ruler of Udaipur, Maharana Bhim Singh; he antagonised the Court at Jodhpur and seems to have completely misjudged Man Singh; he backed the wrong side, the Maharao, in the dispute over succession in Kotah which was won by the Regent, Zalim Singh, with the support of the British. He was seen as too close to the queen mother at Bundi.

It could be said that he behaved with arrogance and failed to obey his superiors, but it does have to be remembered that communication would have been slow and difficult and there must have been many occasions when he had to make decisions on his own. Sometimes that went well, for example gaining control of Kumbalgarh. On other occasions, such as supporting the Maharao of Kotah, it put him at odds with the British. A brief analysis such as this cannot begin to address this difficult question.

Tod's legacy is not in doubt: the *Annals* have never been out of print since 1826 and have been translated into numerous languages, including many Indian languages. They are still regarded as a valid source of information about Rajasthan.

Dr Elizabeth Driver *began her career in cancer research before becoming a lawyer working on pharmaceutical and medical device litigation. Her interest in Indian history, art and culture goes back many years and she has been a member of the Council of the Royal Asiatic Society since 2010. A chance meeting with a descendant of Col. James Tod led to a desire to know more about this enigmatic figure.*

ABOUT THE THIRD VOLUME OF THE *ANNALS AND ANTIQUITIES OF RAJASTHAN*
To commemorate its bicentenary, the Royal Asiatic Society has commissioned a limited edition re-issue of Lt Col James Tod's *Annals and Antiquities of Rajasthan*, with a new companion volume by Norbert Peabody. Tod was a founding member of the Society and its first librarian. While librarian, he completed his *Annals*, originally published in 1829 and 1832, in two volumes. The third volume contains new scholarship by Norbert Peabody in the form of notes and explanations of the original text, essays setting the context for the book and its subsequent history, (it has never, in one form or another, been out of print) and over 170 reproductions of drawings, engravings and paintings from the Royal Asiatic Society's own collection, most of which have never been published before.

—∞—

REFERENCES
1. Lt-Col James Tod, *The Annals and Antiquities of Rajasthan*, Oxford University Press (1920).
2. Jason Freitag, *Serving Empire, Serving Nation: James Tod and the Rajputs of Rajasthan*, Brill (2009), p. 4.
3. Freitag *Serving Empire*, p. 52.
4. Giles Tillotson Personal Communication and see G.R.H Tillotson, *The Rajput Palaces: The Development of an Architectural Style*, Yale University Press (1987).
5. Lt-Col James Tod, *Travels in Western India*, Wm. H Allen 1839.
6. Freitag, *Serving Empire*, pp. 38-40.

COMINGS AND GOINGS: THE ROYAL ASIATIC SOCIETY IN CHINA

By Peter Hibbard

ABSTRACT

The North China Branch of the Royal Asiatic Society (NCBRAS) was established in Shanghai by British and American residents in the late 1850s, growing and flourishing over the following nine decades, until war and political upheaval caused the Society to close its doors in 1952. Almost sixty years later, a group of expatriate residents in Eastern China cautiously attempted to re-establish the Society. The first President of the new venture, now called the Royal Asiatic Society Shanghai in China, Peter Hibbard, describes some of the challenges, successes, people and events of this period.

I felt no small measure of trepidation and hesitancy, when I provisionally accepted the role of presidency of the reinstated Royal Asiatic Society (RAS) Shanghai branch in mid-2007. Apart from other wider issues I asked myself if I actually wanted to do it, was I the right person to do it and was I confident enough and able to do it. It really was a time for reflection on where I was in life. I had always been a part-time nomad, predicated by a very deprived childhood, never being set on a career nor driven by material reward. I had always followed my interests and passions and my interest in China tourism took me to Hong Kong University in December 1985 and into the mainland soon after. I first visited Shanghai in February 1986 when I stayed in a dormitory at the Pujiang Hotel (formerly the glorious and historic Astor House Hotel) and lived in the city in the early 1990s, following a four year sojourn in Beijing. I visited Shanghai over 70 times from the UK over the rest of that decade, returning to live there again and begin a new life in 2001.

Although I had done much research on the development of modern Shanghai, I still had lots to learn and spent many long days at the Bibliotheca Zi-ka-wei, which housed historical books and journals including those of the original North China Branch of the Royal Asiatic Society (NCBRAS). I also made extensive use of the newly opened Shanghai Municipal Archives. It gave me immense pleasure to share my passions and knowledge with others as I hosted historical interpretation tours of Shanghai for inquiring individuals, dignitaries and companies, and gave talks on my work. Adopting the moniker *The Ginger Griffin*, I made it my mission to promote awareness, understanding and appreciation of Shanghai's unique historical inheritance. In 2007 Odyssey had just published my book on the Shanghai Bund[1] and environs, including historical information on the NCBRAS. Through my work, I had built up a fantastic group of friends and also a range of influential contacts. I never purposely pursued or courted such 'society', it just occurred as I went about pursuing my ambitions to learn more and to promote Shanghai. That, I thought, wasn't a bad base from which to start a new adventure.

With the decision made, it was full steam ahead on a journey through what were the best four years of my life.

In fact it wasn't really a new adventure as I realised that I was actually functioning as a conduit to the past. We weren't starting anew, just continuing a story and a dialogue in the same place at a different time.

Thus this essay begins with some essential historical context—to the point where past and present converge with my first meeting of a representative of the RAS at the Bibliotheca Zi-ka-wei in May 2007. It is far from a comprehensive account of what followed. I have merely attempted to outline my vision, trace key developments and recount important highlights and my most memorable experiences, and there were many, within my tenure as president and beyond. Moreover, I hope it speaks of passion, commitment, contentment, joy, friendships and wonderful memories for all those involved.

Once Upon a Time

The first branch of the Royal Asiatic Society of Great Britain & Ireland to establish itself in China opened in Hong Kong in 1847. By its own admonition the Society was 'dogged to some extent' by personal animosities and following the death of Dr. W. A. Hartland, Colonial Surgeon and Secretary and the departure of Sir John Bowring, Hong Kong Governor and President, the Society collapsed in 1859. The Society never found its own premises, but did succeed in publishing six volumes of its *Transactions* over its 12 year history.[2]

Meanwhile, hundreds of miles up the China Coast, Shanghai was fast establishing itself as an emergent global city. Tens of thousands of Chinese flooded into its English settlement, which from 1854 provided sanctuary and security from the ravages of the Taiping Rebellion.

Displaced merchants and intelligentsia of East and West were deposited in the city—though for the time being their circumstances, motives, ambitions and their worlds were poles apart. A new cultural milieu and order was created as two civilisations collided in close physical proximity. The foreign, largely British community, contained many members who were making huge fortunes on the back of contraband trade in opium, but in addition to profiting from the might of China, recognised their ignorance of the nation that now housed them. This recognition fuelled a quest for a new paradigm of understanding beyond their own self-interests in commerce or religion.

That journey began on 24 September 1857 when a group of 18 British and American residents assembled at the Masonic Hall on the Bund to form the Shanghai Literary and Scientific Society. At its first meeting on October 16, the president Dr. Elijah Coleman Bridgman, the first American missionary to reach China in 1830, precipitously foretold that Shanghai would soon become 'one of the greatest centres of interest and of influence, perhaps the greatest, in the Eastern hemisphere,' believing that 'literature and science must surely find a nursery and a home here'. He envisaged the establishment of a journal, a library and a museum as instruments in progressing the society's aims of investigating China and the surrounding nations.

Little time was wasted in starting a lecture series and reproducing their content in the Society's first journal, published in June 1858, with articles on meteorology, numismatics, Buddhism, Japan and Sino-foreign relations. In the previous month the Royal Asiatic Society of Great Britain and Ireland in London had approved the organisation's request for affiliation under the name of the North China Branch of the Royal Asiatic Society (NCBRAS). That request was ratified at a meeting in Shanghai on 26 October 1858. Despite donations of books and collectors' items from the outset, the development of a library and a museum would have to wait as momentum was lost following Bridgman's death in 1861. Sir Harry Parkes, the British Consul in Shanghai and subsequently British Minister to China, enthusiastically resuscitated the Society in 1864. Parkes was the first of twelve British and one American Consuls who would assume presidency of the organisation. The Society began to fully realise its ambitions when it was granted a plot of land in 1868, whereupon an unpretentious two-storey building designed by Thomas Kingsmill, RAS Council member and later president, was completed in late 1871. The RAS library moved in 1872 and the museum collection (consisting largely of stuffed birds) in 1874.

Shanghai again experienced a period of spectacular growth and development in the 1920s and 1930s. Importantly, Arthur de Carle Sowerby, museum director and later president, spearheaded the development of the Society, including a new building for its library and expanded museum during these years. He held massive ambitions for the Society and for the arts in Shanghai. He asked 'who ever heard of a city (except Shanghai) with a population running into millions not having an art gallery for the exhibition of modern or contemporary paintings?'[3] The Society was extremely fortunate in having George Leopold Wilson, Shanghai's pre-eminent British architect, the architect responsible for numerous grand buildings on the Shanghai Bund and beyond, on its Council. Wilson had been on the Council since 1927[4] and designed the magnificent new NCBRAS art deco building on the site of its former premises at 20 Huqiu Road that opened in early 1933.

Whilst the outbreak of the Second Sino-Japanese War in 1937 saw a fall-off in membership as many fled the city, the 12,000-volume library was hosting record numbers of readers, largely Chinese professors and students denied the use of their own facilities. In addition, Sowerby steered the Society towards financial security by housing the American-financed International Institute of China's museum and library on its premises in 1940, which encouraged even more local social acceptance. Over 45,000 visitors to the museum, largely Chinese school children, were recorded in 1939. That figure grew to over 65,000 in 1940[5], and the Society was looking towards a future of security and promise.

However, Sowerby's life and that of the RAS were turned head-over-heels with the Japanese occupation of the city in December 1941. Ironically, in its guise as a Sino-Japanese cultural centre, the museum received more visitors than ever before; and the library collection, which had been augmented by 4,000 volumes from the International Institute in 1940, swelled again as private and institutional collections, including those of the Japanese authorities, found a new home there. Up to two-thirds of the library's contents, including its newspaper and periodical collection, were moved to Tokyo in 1943, but many were returned following the war.

The NCBRAS published its final journal in 1948 and was formally dissolved in May 1952 when its assets, including the library, were given by consent to the government of the People's Republic of China. Despite speculation that the library collection had been lost or destroyed, it was absorbed into the Shanghai Municipal Library in 1955 and housed at the Bibliotheca Zi-ka-wei, which to my glee opened to the public in 2003.

In the Beginning—the RAS Hangzhou Branch

It was within its wonderfully atmospheric reading room on 31 May 2007 that I met with Dr. Judith Kolbas, Vice-President of RAS London and founding president of its Hangzhou branch, which was initiated in October 2005. It was an informal, exploratory, visit during which she hoped to ascertain access to the collection and consider matters related to its conservation and appreciation of what was a rare collection, many volumes of which weren't held at the British Library.

I had long known that the Society's library had survived the ravages of the Cultural Revolution. In the late 1980s and early 1990s, the reading room of the Shanghai Public Library was housed in the former premises of the Shanghai Race Club on People's Square. I described my personal experience of looking at newspapers, periodical and books stamped with the seal of the North China Branch of the Royal Asiatic Society to Judith. Some of the volumes were transported to me by taxi or bicycle from our current location, some eight kilometres away.

Wang Renfang, my friend and director of the library, gave us a private tour of the NCBRAS collection on the floor above the reading room that was strictly out of bounds to the public. Hoping to find support for the restoration of the collection, Judith approached the British Library, and received a favourable response—but an initiative would have to come from Shanghai and that, unsurprisingly, never

Figure 1 & 2: The RAS Library in 1941 and 2012.

materialised. When the Society was resurrected in Shanghai we attempted dialogue on the matter of conservation, but it became clear that this was a sensitive issue that was best not pursued. I believed that the collection was in good hands and that maintaining good relations with the Shanghai Municipal Library might prove to be beneficial in the future. Indeed the library later provided the support we needed for the restoration of some of our own historical journals, as well as digitising and publishing a full set of the NCBRAS journals.

The Hangzhou branch of the Society, had made a decision to move its activities to its birthplace, a decision prompted by Judith's imminent return to the USA. Members held their first Council meeting in Shanghai on 23 May 2007. I was asked to take on the role of president in the near future. Partly surprised, honoured and somewhat bemused I tacitly and provisionally accepted, though I returned home contemplative of what this would mean for me and my family. Others at that meeting included Hangzhou vice-presidents, Dr. Liu Wei and Justin O'Jack of Zhejiang University and their treasurer Mike Nethercott, as well as Dr. Lindsay Shen, an outstanding Shanghai-based scholar and Tess Johnston, author/Shanghai icon who like myself had been invited along as prospective Council members.

My main concerns surrounded the legitimacy and acceptability of reconvening a former institution that still had a palpable physical and emotional presence in the city.

Apart from the library, numerous artefacts from the NCBRAS museum had been moved to the Shanghai Natural History Museum, which was housed in the decrepit, but wonderfully intact premises of the 1921 Chinese Cotton Goods Exchange on Central Yan'an Road. The museum opened in 1958. Whilst the objects were preserved, their context was somewhat lost—Sowerby's orderly vision of portraying the cosmos was supplanted by a ramshackle display of exhibits. The giant panda and little Chinese panda that had once inhabited the prize showcases at the RAS Museum were displayed in rather haphazard fashion, but they still brought joy to the faces of its visitors, including that of my young daughter. Sadly, most of the RAS holdings were disposed of following the building's closure in 2009.

However, the most prominent and visceral reminder of the Society's past importance in the city stood proud and tall in the form of its building still bearing inscriptions of the Society's name in English and Chinese. The building, latterly occupied by a bank, then vacant and neglected, was awaiting a new career as part of a major regeneration project of a small number of buildings, with the NCBRAS building among them. I was fortunate in being involved, having spent many happy hours exchanging information and ideas with Ben Wood, the famed American architect in charge of the project. When visiting the NCBRAS building on frequent occasions during this process I was pleased to see that its integrity and numerous original features had survived. Clearly the building held great importance for the Shanghai authorities.

Judith had recounted with some trepidation, that the society had operated in Hangzhou along the lines of an informal "supper club":

I went to the local police station to notify them of our organisation. The officer just shook his head, nodded, and did not take any notes, Dr. Liu commented that the police were being lenient. Nevertheless, for the next couple of years, I was prepared to be expelled from the country at short notice.

With the move to Shanghai, Judith was keen to explore one last avenue, having set up a meeting with the CEO of HSBC on 3 July to see if the Society could open an account. It proved out of the question as the Society had no legal status. Simply, there was no route to formal recognition (as an NGO or independent body) by the authorities. An application form didn't exist! I wasn't willing to move ahead with any public declaration of the Society until I felt comfortable and assured (with the same applying to any regulatory authorities involved) that such a move wouldn't in anyway jeopardise the venture.

Working with Mike Nethercott on this delicate issue we turned to Ian Crawford, director of the British Chamber of Commerce for assistance. Whilst the British Chamber in Beijing had formal recognition it wasn't so in Shanghai, resulting in Ian attending monthly meetings with representatives of the Public Security Bureau (PSB). His initial efforts to explain our situation were met with silence, but on 21 August I received an email from him stating 'there will be no problem coming concerning our presence in Shanghai.' That I was overcome with massive sense of relief, optimism and gratitude was an understatement. I, along with Ian, attended a meeting with the PSB in the following week to register our existence, show our credentials and put forward our plans, and was told 'we are pleased to see you back,' and that they would 'assist us in registering as a society with the proper City authorities.'

Behind the scenes Mike Nethercott, Dr. Lindsay Shen, Justin O'Jack and Dr. Kim Taylor, myself and Tom Lear who assisted in technical and design matters, had been very busy in anticipation of such approval. There was a lot to ponder—from the technicalities of setting up an effective communication system, building up a membership base, finding venues and contacting potential speakers to broad matters of planning, policy and promotion. Jeffrey Wang, one of Mike Nethercott's staff, provided invaluable help.

Before my involvement with RAS, I had been a member of Save Shanghai Heritage, another voluntary association that held meetings at the German Consulate. Fellow member, good friend and tour de force, Michelle Blumenthal, helped out with promoting our activities, though couldn't commit to more until her obligation to that organisation came to an end in the following year. Another member of that group, Spencer Dodington, also played an important role in the RAS. Most importantly Carma Elliot OBE, British Consul in Shanghai, kindly agreed to become our Honorary Vice President. Later, in 2009, the British Consulate graciously made a substantial donation towards costs for the redesign of our website.

Whilst the activities of the Hangzhou branch were formally handed over to the Shanghai branch at the meeting on 23 May 2007, the Hangzhou group already had in place two further lectures at the Deke Erh Art Center on Tai Kang Road, facilitated by my dear friend Tess Johnston, (Deke Erh was Tess's collaborator and photographer on her numerous books). The first lecture, by Paolo Sabbatini, examining the life and work of Matteo Ricci, took place following the 23 May meeting. Therein Judith presented to me an heirloom Chinese vase as a token of the president's position. She 'hoped it would be passed on to the next president and those thereafter.' I had the great pleasure of passing it on to Katy Gow, my successor, in 2011. However, the vase and the incumbent president, Nenad Djordjevic, mysteriously vanished into thin air sometime after my departure from Shanghai in 2013. I believe their whereabouts are still unknown. My dear friend Nenad, where are you now?

The next and final 'transitional' lecture/presentation by Jane Portal of the Victoria and Albert Museum and Beth McKillop of the British Museum, who were planning a joint exhibition with the Shanghai Municipal Museum, took place on 24 June.

I delivered my inaugural lecture, 'Beyond the Bund,' exploring the vicinity of the NCBRAS building, at the same venue on 21 October 2007. That date marked the formal return of the first iteration of the Society to the city. Remarkably in the same week, 150 years earlier, president Bridgman presented his inaugural lecture. Continuing the "supper club" principle, we applied a 50 RMB charge for coffee or tea for members and 80 RMB charge for non-members.

With the two-stage conception of the branch complete, echoing that of another ghost from the past—RAS Hong Kong was reformed in 1959, a full century after its demise. History had come full circle.

AND SO IT CAME TO PASS   THE RAS RESURRECTION IN SHANGHAI

I was acutely aware of the need to build upon the Society's fine tradition and to take on some of the challenges and opportunities it faced before its dissolution. The Society was often described as a dry as dust institution, or some such hyperbole, and efforts by former presidents to greater engage the Shanghai public had at best been met with limited success. Just like the former heady years of the 1850/60s and 1920/30s, Shanghai had entered a period of spectacular growth in the early 1990s, attracting a huge influx of people from around the world. It was yet again one of the most of the exciting cities on the planet to live in, with an avaricious hunger for art and culture. New art galleries and museums appeared to be opening weekly and entertainment venues, bars and eateries proliferated. Propitious times.

Whilst I wanted to stay true to the historic tradition of delivering a monthly, or regular 'lecture' of a scholastic nature, I wished to massively broaden the scope of the society to reflect and embrace the rich cultural milieu in which we found ourselves and draw upon the passions and interests of our diverse multi-cultural community.

I attempted to reflect this in our original mission statement: 'to provide a forum for the development and expression of interests and expertise from within the local community, and from around the globe, to inspire and to enrich cultural life in Asia's most dynamic metropolis.'

Whilst Shanghai's geographical position obviously hadn't changed, the name—the North China Branch of the RAS—required somewhat of a perceptual shift to be applied today. I did consider keeping the original name as a matter of historical continuity as we simply reconvened the activities of the former branch. However it was a wider geographical ambition that informed my choice of the title 'Royal Asiatic of Society China in Shanghai.' I foresaw that other Chinese cities with foreign

Figure 3: Tess Johnston, the author, and Hong Kong RAS president Robert Nield at the Royal Asiatic Society in Suzhou opening in 2011.

populations might also be encouraged to establish 'chapters' of RAS China, in which case, 'in Shanghai' would be supplanted by their location. And so it came to pass with the establishment of the Royal Asiatic Society in Suzhou on 6 March 2011 under the vice-presidency of Bill Dodson. Tess Johnston gave an opening talk, followed by congratulatory remarks by Robert Nield, who was president of RAS Hong Kong, and myself. Following this development, 'and beyond' was appended to our mission statement.

The Suzhou Society's life was relativity short-lived, but the next venture to Beijing proved more enduring and fulfilled a long held ambition of the NCBRAS. Whilst the NCBRAS had enjoyed a brief affiliation with the Peking Oriental Society, in which key figures in the founding of the NCBRAS Thomas Edkins and Sir Harry Parkes, were involved in the 1880s, subsequent attempts to establish branches or affiliate societies there failed to succeed. The matter was again raised by John Ferguson, president, at a meeting of the Society in June 1911 when he noted the dangers of relying on the activities of any one individual carrying the Society forward and a wish to organise branches at Hong Kong, Hankou and Beijing. Latterly at the 1914 AGM Sir Everard Fraser, president, expressed the desire to encourage the 'formation of a special section of the society as many members lived there' and would also 'be productive of interesting papers for the Journal. It was hoped that this system might be extended to other parts of China later on.'[6]

It took a while, but the Royal Asiatic Society, Beijing, (RASBJ) with

Alan Babington-Smith as president was formally launched on 11 April 2013, starting as a chapter of RAS China in Shanghai. I was extremely proud to be at the event just before my return to UK alongside RAS president Katy Gow. Special credit must be given to the inimitable Paul French for his initiative and outstanding facilitation skills for the ventures in both Suzhou and Beijing. The RASBJ became an independent branch of the Royal Society of Great Britain and Ireland on 6 December, 2018.

As an historian it was procedural for me to connect the past with the present. From the outset I was eager to build up a database of all those connected with the Society since its inception. Not only would this open a window on how the Society, its members and their environment developed over time, it could also provide a useful research tool for those who had Shanghai connections in the past, as well as researchers and the general public. I wanted people to know and understand the important contributions made by many of our members and envisaged that this would be accessible as part of a heritage project on our website, which was still under development in early 2008.

With assistance of James Li, who put in an extraordinary amount of work until his return to the USA in 2010, a database of over 3,100 NCBRAS members was finally compiled, with basic details such as nationality, work place, occupation, residence and membership dates of most members, as well as more biographical information, including photographs and documents, where these could be found. I managed to assemble a substantial amount of information on our more prominent members.

Unfortunately this project was left incomplete and never found a home on our website. However it can be accessed in our Shanghai library and I hope it can be revived in the future.

As a case in point to its potential value, in 2009 I received an email through our enquiry box from Michael Wilson, the grandson of George Leopold Wilson, the aforementioned architect of the NCBRAS building and major figure in Shanghai society, asking if we knew anything of him—as they didn't at all! I was pleased to share what I knew and absolutely overwhelmed when I had the pleasure of escorting him and three family members, including daughter Nina on a tour of Wilson's triumphs including the NCBRAS building and the Peace (Cathay) Hotel in April 2010. As I reported in our May newsletter, 'I am pleased to say that one of the highlights of my tenure as president took place last month. It was a very joyful day and I am so proud to

Figure 4: "Tug" the Society's logo, developed from a photograph of one of the stone lions gracing the roof of the former RAS building. The lions can still be seen from the street today.

think that it was all made possible because of the re-emergence of our Society.' I later received an email from Nina, saying that following her Shanghai experience her newborn son was named George after his great-great grandfather.

I had long held a great admiration for Mr. Wilson, affectionately known as Tug Wilson, and his important contribution to the development of the city and to the enrichment of its cultural and civic life. I decided that our logo adopted from one of a pair of granite lions atop the NCBRAS building, cementing past and present, should be named in his honour—Tug the Lion.

On other procedural matters, we based our Constitution on the London model, with a range of honorary Council (as our committee was known) positions, which would be open to annual election. As reliance on one individual had proved problematic in the past I decided that the post of president could only be held for a maximum of four years, but that he/she would automatically remain on Council thereafter. It was a poignant concern in that Judith had plans to return to the USA in 2006, but choose to remain another year following a 'caution' by Justin O'Jack that her departure would threaten the Society's momentum.

Our first elected Council, in October 2008 consisted of myself (President), Mike Nethercott, Justin O'Jack (Vice-Presidents), Jan Flohr (Honorary Treasurer), Michelle Blumenthal (Honorary Activities Coordinator), Lindsay Shen, Janet Roberts (Honorary Editors), Kim Taylor (Honorary Librarian), with Spencer Dodington, Mike Bradley, Howard Scott and Hugues Martin as Council Members.

Foremost among the other major tasks and longer term projects, true to the original society's aims, was the development of a new library and the reinstatement of our previously esteemed annual journal, as well as other publications. We had no intention of resurrecting the museum—though if the opportunity arose it certainly would have been considered.

The path ahead was clear to me and surrounded by a wonderful, talented, enthusiastic team in the organisation, as well as a tremendously dedicated group of young Chinese volunteers including Jennifer Wen, Stephen Cunsong and Catherine Yin, the journey to bring the Society back to life continued apace.

RAS ACTIVITIES—NEW VENTURES
THE RAS SOIREE

Apart from the lecture series, activities encouraging greater interactivity with our members and guests began in style on 11 December 2007 at the Figaro Coffeehouse, a café in Xintiandi. It was there that we resurrected the RAS Annual Soirée, first held in December 1938 by Arthur de Carle Sowerby to bring new life into the Society, where refreshments and sandwiches were served and a 'motion picture' shown. I was fortunate to know R. E. Barnes, the closest surviving relative of Sir Victor Sassoon and was able hold a private screening of movie clips, largely shot in Shanghai in the 1930s, taken by the legendary Sir Victor himself. Refreshments, sandwiches and canapés were on offer. It was a very special occasion, bringing together many people who would become stalwarts of the Society, and contribute in so many ways to its future development. Kim, who ran a film production company, documented the event and went on to make documentaries of some our members, including myself and Michelle that would be shown on Shanghai TV, further promoting the Society.

RAS RAMBLES

The next new venture took place on 19 January 2008 when I lead the first in a series of walks, which I titled RAS Rambles, in the Waitanyuan district. Again it was a special day as heavy snow fell and we made the most of being granted special access by the Rockbund group to the NCBRAS building by engaging in a snowball josh on its roof! Not so dry as dust now, I chuckled.

Mike Nethercott and Dr. Liu Wei had dug deep into their pockets to secure 79 precious volumes of the RAS North China Branch (Shanghai) Journals dating from 1859 to 1948, to form the nucleus of our new library. Proceeds from the walk would go towards their procurement. I believe that an agreement was later made which signified that they would be kept in perpetuity by the society, but recalled if they were ever under threat. As such, the volumes remain as a gracious loan. Income from some of my later walks was used to pay for the restoration of some of those journals.

Such interpretive walks became a key feature of a whole range of RAS programme events, which apart from myself were lead by our members, notable among them Duncan Hewitt, Bill Savadove, Nenad Djordevic, Michelle Blumenthal, Spencer Dodington. Betty Barr, Lindsay Shen, Tess Johnston and Lynn Pan. It was a privilege and joy to live in such a wonderfully inspiring community at that time. Of those original members, who supported the venture throughout my presidency and beyond, I would like to make a special mention of dear friends Jo Wood and Luise Scahfer OBE.

THE RAS STUDIO

In an attempt to draw upon the interests of that community we came up with the concept of the 'RAS Studio' to denote a more informal gathering in which members and guests could participate. I informed our members by email 'that we have instituted the RAS Studio as a platform for members, visitors and the wider Shanghai community to make a contribution to Shanghai's cultural life. We envisage a varied format of discussions, seminars, classes and film screenings, amongst a host of other activities, which will allow participants to engage over time with topics in a more informal, exploratory way that takes full advantage of the dynamic and talented community in which we live.'

At the first such event on 18 March at Figaro, Nenad Djordjevic, the Serbian Consul and an Honorary Vice President, vividly brought to life two years of dedicated and loving research on old Shanghai societies and associations. We often met, buried behind books at the Bibliotheca Zi-ka-wei. That evening brought me immense satisfaction as I could clearly see the important role the Society could play and epitomised what I wanted to see in a gathering—not just a sharing of knowledge, but also an expression of drive and passion that inspired others.

Clearly hitting the brief our second Studio event on 8 April involved the showing of a documentary film, *Beijing Love,* by French filmmaker Oliver Horn, about two young lovers in Beijing in the 1990s. That was followed on 8 May by a talk on beekeeping in China, Japan and Korea, including a honey tasting session, by John Hamilton a British professor who taught at a law faculty in a Japanese university. It remains one of the most fascinating and interesting talks that I can recall over my entire presidency, embodying novelty, surprise and an eclecticism that again made me feel so proud to be part of the organisation.

A rich assortment of offerings followed over the course of 2008, including presentations by Terry Bennett on photographers

Figure 6: RAS studio event, held in the elegant Figaro Coffee house in 2008. The author stands in front of the screen, with Lindsay Shen and Dr Liu Wei standing to his right.

in Shanghai from 1842 to 1860, Danish family links with Shanghai by Ambassador Christopher Bo Bramsen and our very own Dr. Liu Wei in December with a talk and film about the famous fin-de-siècle courtesan, Sai Jinhua, the Boxers and the 1900 Occupation of Beijing.

Our first lecture was delivered in a meeting room of the historic Pujiang (Astor House) hotel on 30 November 2007. It was more than fitting that it should be given by a Chinese citizen, and a good friend that I had made through my research on his home city. Mr. Zhang Jianguo, director of the Weihai Archives Bureau, Shandong province, told of his experiences spearheading a remarkable project to recover the lost British history of his city that resulted in the development of valuable Sino-British ties and in the publication of a great book, *Weihaiwei under British Rule.* He was assisted that evening by his colleague Ma Xianghong. I am writing this article in Weihai now—having just visited the new Weihai Municipal Archives where Ms. Ma still works (Mr. Zhang having retired). My involvement with the RAS has created many endearing friendships, for which I will forever be grateful.

While the intimate surroundings of the Figaro coffeehouse were perfect for smaller gatherings, including Studio events and some lectures, our first regular large venue suitable for formal lectures was at InterfaceFLOR in Raffles City on People's Square.

The first lecture at InterfaceFLOR on nature and Daoism by Prof. James Miller took place and on 8 January. Among other lectures held there in 2008 we hosted Professor Zu'en of Fudan University who explored Japanese Society in Concession Era Shanghai and RAS Council member Dr Kim Taylor, who delivered a fascinating talk on the extraordinary contribution made by Dr. Wu Liande to epidemic disease prevention in early 20th century China. One of the leading figures in the development of modern medicine in China, Dr. Wu was also a NCBRAS Council member and the financial saviour of the former NCBRAS building. Wonderful to have such expertise at hand.

TWO VERY SPECIAL OCCASIONS AND TWO VERY SPECIAL PEOPLE
Our team had put a lot of effort into making our 150th anniversary celebration in May very special, hoping to attract a large audience and increase our visibility in the city. The date chosen was 17 May, the closest weekend date to when the NCBRAS branch was formally

recognised by the Royal Asiatic Society of Great Britain & Ireland, 150 years and two days earlier (15 May 1858).

I was adamant that I wanted the event to take place in the NCBRAS building and was elated when the Rockbund group agreed to this. However the day after Lindsay had sent out the invitations I received notice that the building had been deemed unfit for use. It was an horrendous shock and I remember chasing around with Lindsay in a furious attempt to find a new venue. In the end we found a magnificent space in Shanghai 1933, a former abattoir of outstanding art deco design, that was being developed by Paul Liu and famed Australian restaurateur David Laris, respectively chairman and creative director of Axons Concepts. I knew Paul as the man responsible for the magnificent reinvention of the Three on the Bund building (where I had recently held a talk). They spontaneously and generously provided the space, all equipment, facilities, staff and catering for free and I remain eternally grateful to them for that 'great escape.'

It was a gloriously sunny day and proceedings began with Jane Portal, Curator of Chinese and Korean collections at the British Museum, on her return to Shanghai, giving a presentation on the British Museum's relations with China, including Shanghai. David Laris made a short speech about the 1933 project and the majestic Carma Elliot OBE finished the afternoon with warm words for us all. The day was resounding success and ended with a walk lead by myself and Jane Portal past the NCBRAS building to Three on the Bund. Around 100 people attended the event.

The next big event, over the weekend 21-24 November, saw the visit of 26 members and two friends of the RAS Hong Kong. It took months of planning and organisation took and I was assisted by Michelle Blumenthal, who had wholeheartedly committed herself to the RAS

Figure 7: The 150th anniversary celebration, held in May 2008, at "Shanghai 1933", a former abattoir with art deco design features. Left to right: British Consul Carma Elliot, Jane Portal, and Katy Gow.

following the summer break. I had drawn up a detailed itinerary for their two and a half day visit, which would begin with a full day tour lead by myself tour exploring the Bund and Waitanyuan area, followed by a special visit to see the restoration work at the former Holy Trinity Cathedral. We were pledged access as I was involved in the project. Following a walk in the lilongs (old lanes) around my home, we would visit the Bibliotheca Zi-ka-wei for a tour of the NCBRAS collection, as well as the former French Jesuit library. Next door at the former St. Ignatius Cathedral we were to meet Michelle to hear about the restoration of its stained glass windows before ending the day with a visit to 1933. Tours of the former French Concession and Pudong would occupy the subsequent days.

All went to plan and was much enjoyed by all. However something extraordinary happened between the planning stage and the day of their arrival. In fact it was an extraordinary person, Pixie Gray, who became a dear friend, who would make that weekend so special, even though she would be far away in Australia when it took place.

Pixie, who was born in Shanghai, first approached me by email in January 2008 as she was curious to know if her old school building had survived, and indeed, if her former home had. A flurry of exchanges followed in advance of her proposed visit with husband John and I was most interested to receive copy of her father's unpublished account of his internment in Shanghai during World War II. She kindly accepted my request to talk about her life in Shanghai and she took me for a stroll around her old haunts in September 2008.

Pixie presented an absorbing and moving account of her family history in China and of her early memories of Shanghai, to a large and appreciative audience on 9 September. She was born at the Paulun Hospital on 19 March 1936 and apart from a sojourn in Hong Kong in 1937, lived in Shanghai till October 1941 when she and her mother and older sister, Elizabeth were sent by their father to Australia prior to the bombing of Pearl Harbour. Her father, Henry Pringle, stayed behind and was imprisoned by the Japanese. The three lived in Australia until late 1946 when they returned to Shanghai. Both girls attended the Shanghai British School until late 1948 when again they fled to Australia. Following the event Pixie donated a digital copy of her father's harrowing account of his captivity in Shanghai and Beijing during the war years to our library. With Pixie's endorsement I posted in our website and entered into discussion with Graham Earnshaw with a view towards publication. Meanwhile Pixie also donated DVDs containing hours of her father's digitised home movies from the 1930s and 1940s to the Society, of which some clips were shown at the event.

It was at that moment that I felt that they deserved to been seen by a wider audience of our members and friends and what better occasion to do that, but upon the visit of our associates from Hong Kong. Thus the second Annual Soirée (and also the 70th anniversary of the NCBRAS event) was incorporated into the weekend event on 22 November. Fortuitously, we had arranged for the group to stay at Astor House (Pujiang Hotel) and Simon Ma, deputy general manager and long-time friend gave us the use of its ballroom, created in 1922 and graciously removed its carpets to expose its wonderfully intricate dance floor for the evening.

To say it was a special evening would very much be an understatement. It was a night of pure joy, with around 100 people in attendance.

I assembled a compilation of dance music from the 1920s to the 1940s to accompany Pixie's movies with the final song being 'Thanks for the Memory' released in 1938 and performed by Bob Hope and Shirley Ross. One vivid memory of that wonderful night was when Mike Nethercott approached me with a beaming smile and said 'Thank you Peter.' In fact I had a lot to thank him and the amazing team around me for in making the first year of activities such a brilliant success, borne of a massive amount of dedication and sheer

Figure 8: The second annual soirée, held in the Astor House ballroom in 2008.

Figure 9: Graham Earnshaw, Pixie and John Gray with copies of *Bridge House Survivor*, a memoir of her father's experiences as a prisoner of war.

hard work.

One of the Hong Kong visitors reported to his Society on return that 'these unique views of her (Pixie's) family life in Shanghai—children playing in the garden, parties and school events, and then the arrival of the Japanese and the subsequent turmoil—were playing on a large screen throughout the evening and made for compulsive viewing.'

I was overjoyed to welcome Pixie and John back to Shanghai in April 2009. John gave the RAS a heartfelt presentation titled 'Shanghai 1942-1945: the Henry Pringle story.' It was a very moving experience and a milestone moment for me as Graham Earnshaw, founder of Earnshaw Books, presented Pixie and John with copies of *Bridge House Survivor: Experiences of a Civilian Prisoner-of-war in Shanghai & Beijing 1942–45*[7] that he had just published. I was so proud that we were able to facilitate its publication in print form and indebted to Graham and his passion for our cause. Graham, apart from supporting and occasionally speaking at our events, would become involved with other RAS projects, notably as publisher of the Society's journal.

The last time that I saw Pixie and John was on 23 March 2010 when they were in Shanghai just for the day and we managed to break though barriers to visit her old school and the former Holy Trinity Cathedral, where she was christened in 1937.

The last major innovation relating to our activities during my presidency was the institution of the RAS Weekender.

Whilst many walks would take place at weekends, Michelle and I felt that we should extend and expand our other activities to that time period, to accommodate those who found difficulty in attending weekday evening events and to appeal to a wider family audience. Most lectures were held on Tuesday evenings.

As I communicated in an email to our membership in January 2009, We hope that Weekenders will provide an opportunity for all —RAS members, their families, friends and guests. to discover and appreciate more about Shanghai's astounding history and culture and [...] we hope that they will be a great deal of fun.

RAS Weekender events were usually of half-day duration, providing a great chance to get together with others over an optional meal or drink in convivial surroundings. Most static events were held in the sumptuous surroundings of the T8 Club Lounge in Xintiandi.

Michelle had organised her first event at that venue on 15 November 2008 with a talk by Elizabeth Gill Lui, author and photographer of the newly released book *Open Hearts Open Doors: Reflections on China's Past and Present.*[8]

Apart from the T8 Club Lounge, Michelle had widened the scope of of venues to include Mesa-Manifesto, The PuLi Hotel and Spa, Sasha's, Melange Oasis, Chai Bites, the Sino-British College, the Radisson Plaza Xing Guo Hotel and M on the Bund, by 2011. The Tavern at the Radisson became a popular and much used venue and thanks must given to Howard Bennett, managing director, for his support of the RAS. Howard and I have a long history going back to working together in Beijing in 1990.

With her infectious verve and voracity Michelle came up with a brilliant series of highly successful monthly events, commencing on 28 February 2009 with a walk examining the history of the clubs and associations of old Shanghai by none other than Nenad Djordevic whose book *Old Shanghai Clubs & Associations* had recently been published by Earnshaw Books.

A bloom of events in the ensuing months included a tour of the botanical gardens with Alison Jefferson, stalwart supporter Betty Barr and some of her alumni of the Shanghai American School telling of their lives and school days before the World War II, an examination of symbols and imagery in Chinese traditional culture at the Shanghai Museum with Helga Brandt Corstius and another RAS stalwart, Mishi Saran, talking about her book *Chasing the Monk's Shadow*.

The umbrella of the RAS Weekender also embraced a number of trips orchestrated by Michelle, including trips to Moganshan, Suzhou and a number of fabulous journeys north to the WildWall, for treks along the Great Wall hosted by the distinguished William Lindsay OBE and his wife Wu Qi. As part of this series I brought to life a trip to my beloved Weihai, a place that I first visited in 1988.

Over the weekend of 23-26 July 2010 I had the pleasure of hosting 12 members on a trip to Weihai. It began with an impromptu stop at Yangting village, where a family spontaneously appeared with a basket of apricots for us and ended at a "Scottish castle" tasting experimental wines and gorging on a four-course dinner (including lamb chops and mint sauce) served in its baronial hall. We were at The Treaty Port Vineyards owned by Shanghai based Chris Ruffle.

In the interim we paid a visit to Yantai (the former treaty port of Chefoo) to see the heart of the former foreign district, with its mix of commercial and diplomatic buildings that still smelled of history.

We had a wonderful visit to the Weihai Municipal Archives, where we were reunited with Mr. Zhang Jianguo, who stepped out of retirement to host us alongside Ma Xianghong. Ms. Ma stayed with us throughout the day, as we visited some villas including one formerly owned by E. S. Wilkinson, a former NCBRAS luminary. In the afternoon we took to the seas for a visit to Liugong Island, the former base of the Chinese, Japanese and British navies.

Boxing Day Walk

I introduced the annual Boxing Day Walk in 2009 when the highlight was a visit to the stacks of the former NCBRAS library. For those not in the know, going for a walk on Boxing Day (26 December) is a peculiar British tradition. It was meant to be an entertaining, yet informative adventure into Shanghai past and present. The 2010 walk, 'A Boxing Day Hunt and a Christmas Carol,' was my most memorable foray. We began by knocking on the doors of some local residents in my neighbourhood who invited us in to sing carols, then discovered the story behind the tombstone of Charles Cathcart, Britain's little recognised first ambassador to China, recently and significantly, uncovered in the wall of the former Holy Trinity Cathedral. The main event was a hunt for some former NCBRAS specimens found in the Natural History Museum. I made photocopies of old photos of some birds, crustaceans and animals in our former museum for each of the 15 strong group, before letting them loose on the chase. It brought back memories of school outings and Easter egg hunts. We ended the day with refreshments at the historic Long Bar of the Waldorf Astoria Hotel, where Arthur de Carle Sowerby installed a collection of animal heads and horns in the 1920s in its original guise as the Shanghai Club. They were long gone.

From the outset I had imagined the formation of various special interest groups under the RAS banner With my particular interest in heritage, I approached Save Shanghai Heritage to adopt our patronage, but they declined, wishing to maintain their distinct identity. The first ventures included the establishment of the RAS Book Club by Alexandra Hendrickson in 2010, the RAS Film Club with Charles Johnson taking the lead, followed by Linda Johnson soon after and the RAS Modern History Study Group with Katie Baker at the helm in 2011. Such ventures were highly successful and helped lessen the burden on Michelle.

Coordinated by Michelle, in her inimitable professional manner, our events programme went from strength to strength—encompassing a rich variety of activities and events, and covering a wide range of topics and interests. Our programme included no less than 30 activities in 2009—with RAS Lectures on topics as diverse as modern dance, Buddhism, studies of Ming and Qing, and Studio presentations on topics ranging from photography and publishing to wartime Shanghai.

THE RAS LIBRARY

As previously highlighted, the library collection could hardly have got off to a better start with the generous loan of the majority of the Society's former journals being secured by Mike Nethercott and Dr. Liu Wei in December 2007. The journals, embracing the rich history of the Society, laid the essential foundations upon which a unique collection highlighting the importance of the former Society could be built upon. As such my primary focus was to expand the collection with material related to the people and activities that made the RAS such an outstanding cultural institution in the past, as well as representing the works of those involved with Society today, again linking past and present. I envisaged building up a special collection of their works and showcasing them in a section of our future library.

I thought the best place to start was to search for the works of key figures, former presidents. librarians and recognised scholars, who were once members of the Society. The journals themselves were a great resource as they contained name lists. As I was already familiar with his role in the Society and some of his publications, my attentions turned to Arthur de Carle Sowerby, the most important person in the development of the Society in the 20th century. A visit to the Smithsonian Institution in Washington DC allowed me explore his archive, and I returned to Shanghai with a huge amount of material, among them piles of photocopies and a wonderful assortment of digital images (taken on my first digital camera). I hoped, that alongside the database of NCBRAS members this would form the core of our 'heritage' project to be housed in the library, and would later find digital representation on our evolving website.

As with the original formation of NCBRAS it would take some while before permanent premises open to members and visitors would be found for the ever expanding collection, with gifts from past speakers and our membership. Stephen Cunsong painstakingly compiled a catalogue the journals contents and I set about digitising all of its 'proceedings' telling of the Society's activities, as well as making copies of numerous relevant or important articles therein, again with a view to posting on the website at a later date, or perhaps making a compilation book.

From the outset we were eager to foster relations with kindred Societies just as the NCBRAS had done. In the 19th century they had relations with many organisations in Europe, as well as with the American Oriental Society, which not only allowed an exchange of ideas, but of books and journals as well. To this end Mike Nethercott met with Great Britain & Ireland Council members in London in January 2008 to discuss our vision for the sharing knowledge and resources and announced that 'we plan to network with all existing RAS branches to promote our mutual aim of better appreciating and understanding Asian cultures.' Three valuable copies of our journal from around 1900, previously missing from our collection, donated by Mr. J. Leach of London, were handed over to Mike by Dr. Alison Ohta, the Society's curator. Following the publication my review of the Society's activities that appeared in the RAS London Spring

Newsletter 2008 further donations were received. In early 2009 RAS Hong Kong generously donated an entire collection of their journals dating from 1960. Thereafter we reciprocated with Hong Kong in an exchange of our journals. Council member Charles Johnson worked on fostering contacts with other RAS branches in Asia in 2011.

Kim Taylor had wished to take on the role developing the library since its inception and was duly elected as honorary librarian in 2008. She had overseen the growth of the library that one year later had perhaps tripled in volume with a collection of 81 books and 119 journals and begun the painstaking task of cataloguing them and posted details on our website. There were numerous donations including those from Tess Johnston, Lynn Pan and Paul French. I identified one rare book as a 'must' and was fortunate to procure and donate a copy of Arthur de Carle Sowerby's *China's Natural History: A Guide to the Shanghai Museum (R.A.S.)*[9].

Kim used funds raised for the library in the restoration of 24 old journals and in late 2009 managed the move to our first premises that could provide public access at CIEE, East China Normal University. With this development a new drive to expand the library began with an appeal to membership for donations in published and digital formats.

In pursuit of a more central location and more convivial surroundings to encourage more visitors the Council agreed to move the library to the Waldorf Astoria Hotel on the Bund, the former Shanghai Club, in early 2011. The upcoming move was announced at the Society's AGM in November 2010 held in the palatial surroundings of the hotel. The library was to be moved into a magnificent space formerly occupied Club's prestigious library. I was keen to represent our history in the hotel where I had recently been charged with the task of naming its restaurants and function rooms. I named its American restaurant Pelham's in honour of Sir Warren Pelham who opened the building in 1911 and was an influential NCBRAS president in the early 20th century.

Kim and Michelle put in an enormous amount of work to enable the move, which was not without a hitch as some boxes of books disappeared in transit, never to be recovered. The next 'core' collection of journals built up within the library was that of the fascinating *The China Journal* established in 1923 and edited by Arthur de Carle Sowerby, until 1937. Tess, myself and Spencer had individually amassed a large collection of the journals purchased in a Shanghai second hand market where they curiously appeared week after week. We also decided to donate all our copies to the library.

However, despite the glamour, the apparent sense and the 'historical correctness,' of the move to the Waldorf I had a deep sense of unease as the year progressed. Issues related to security and access for our members proliferated. At a Council meeting in September 2011, one of my last meetings as president of the Society, Kim had found the management uncooperative and 'more interested in the aesthetic value of the Collection than in it having any functional use.' Furthermore locks supposedly guarding our rare books were not fit for purpose and an entire cabinet of archive material and other papers had mysteriously disappeared (but these were later tracked down). We had little control over the safekeeping of the collection and a decision was made to move the library to the Sino-British College instead.

Enormous gratitude must be accorded to Professor Ian Gow OBE, (husband of the new president Katy Gow) Principal at the Sino-British College (SBC), for providing a perfectly proportioned annex next to the main library for our collection. The College also provided much needed administrative support and the room would double up as an RAS office. Kim graciously agreed to stay on as Honorary Librarian to organise the move.

Alongside Kim, Ed Allen (Honorary Librarian-elect), Anya Thomsen, Ian Crawford and others assisted with the mammoth task of cataloguing a large amount of new acquisitions, mostly donations. Tess Johnston made a substantial and valuable donation of books, journals and research material. With my departure from Shanghai not too far away I also donated many books as well as a digital record of my voluminous research and records on the Society from over the years. This included print copies of records relating to the Society including those from the Shanghai Municipal Archives to accompany Sowerby's archive. Numerous DVDs, including Victor Sassoon's and Pixie Gray's movies already formed part of the collection.

A soft opening of the library to a select group of invitees took place on 24 June 2012, with the official opening on 26 October. It was a truly momentous occasion as we had a library we could rightfully call our own for the first time in over 60 years.

Figure 10: Authors Duncan Hewitt and Paul French inspect the collection with Katy Gow at the library opening in 2012, in the Sino-British College.

PUBLICATIONS

THE **RAS** MONTHLY NEWSLETTER

Whilst I had kept members and friends up to date with RAS matters and other relevant information with an occasional newsletter in simple Word format, I had long wished to have a more professional monthly missive. That wish was made possible when Katy Gow was 'co-opted' to take on the role of honorary secretary in December 2009. Katy, a prominent figure in the voluntary sector and fundraiser for many worthy causes was also president of Brits Abroad, Shanghai. With her wonderfully effervescent personality, genial authority and organisational genius, she wasted little time in producing a marvellous, richly illustrated newsletter in the following month.

In my speech at the November 2010 AGM (a copy of which appeared in the December newsletter), I remarked that Katy 'jumped in at the deep-end, taking on the demanding role of Honorary Secretary, a key function in the Society, and immediately set about launching our much needed newsletter, giving order and direction to meetings and proceedings, and bringing smiles all around.'

Apart from its value as a communication tool the newsletter offered future chroniclers, like myself right now, a great insight into the development and activities of the Society. Whilst the NCBRAS didn't have a newsletter letter as such, full accounts of its activities from 1857 on were recorded in the pages of the *North China Herald*, Shanghai's leading British newspaper. I managed to extract all such references from the paper in PDF format up to the mid-1920s and these along with copies of the newsletter are to be found in our library.

THE JOURNAL OF THE ROYAL ASIATIC SOCIETY IN SHANGHAI

The revival of this crucially important journal was spearhead by Lindsay Shen, who stoically took on the on the role of honorary secretary, but stepped down in late 2008. She was predestined to use her astounding ability and creativity in bringing history to life in the form of our new journal. The long and arduous process she engaged in with Janet Roberts, as co-editor, not without some friction, resulted in the launch of the journal in May 2010, 62 years following the date of its last publication.

Bearing the cover design of the NCBRAS journal faithfully reproduced by Earnshaw Books and fastidiously edited by Derek Sandhaus, the first journal bore the title Volume 74, No. 1 April 2010, causing some librarians to stutter and think why there was such a massive gap in years when placing it on their library shelves.

In its preface we remarked that

[…] this new chapter of the journals existence will, we trust, be shaped by relentless curiosity and innovative scholarship [...] It is the ambition of the Society that its journal should once again be a repository of outstanding scholarship on historic and contemporary China.[10]

Two major NCBRAS figures were investigated in the journal. Lindsay wrote on *Florence Ayscough in Shanghai: Interpreting China though Autobiography**, while I penned a piece titled *Unanswered Questions: Notes on the Life of Arthur de Carle Sowerby*. I wrote of the man himself—his adventures, triumphs, troubles, and foibles, based on his archived material that I had been so fortunate to explore. I felt so much empathy.

RAS CHINA MONOGRAPH SERIES

Apart from its journal the NCBRAS rarely ventured into publishing its own material. That void was filled when the inimitable Paul French became involved with the Society. I had come to know Paul over an exchange of notes on Shanghai history in 2007. He was a regular attendee and occasional, and hugely popular, speaker at our events and made major contributions to our library. Paul's numerous approaches to the Society from 2008 on, with his introductions to potential speakers, contacts and thoughts on its development, particularly in the publication arena, were a breath of fresh air. I recall numerous meetings over an evening drink, usually accompanied by Michelle, that eventually resulted in an agreement for him to develop a truly exciting book series, subtitled *China Monographs* in association with the Hong Kong University Press.

Paul joined the RAS Council as Honorary Research and Publications Director (an appellation I came up with especially for him) in 2009 to initiate the project. He noted that while other RAS branches tend to produce longer, more traditional academic books, the aim for the RAS China branch should be to produce a series of shorter, more tightly focussed books. This format would attract a wider range of writers beyond academics and professional authors, in order to draw out existing knowledge and research currently not being published.

The books, from around 20,000 to 25,000 words in length, were to be affordable, with 'subject areas to be as broad as defined by the RAS China Council and include history, society, literature, biography, arts and culture.'[11]

Paul's gargantuan efforts in reasserting the Society's academic pedigree and offering opportunities for scholars and writers in finding an audience bore fruit in October 2012 with the publication of Dr. Lindsay Shen's *Knowledge is Pleasure: A Life of Florence Ayscough*[12] that was launched at the aforementioned RAS library opening at SBC. Our next publication was by Professor Anne Witchard, *Lao She in London*[13], which was launched on 13 November at the RAS Suzhou chapter and in Shanghai on the eighteenth of that month. More were to follow.

Paul has made regular ongoing contributions to the Society's journal and I remain extremely grateful for his work in initiating a fascinating publication series.

THE NCBRAS BUILDING

With the mantle passed from Ben Wood to the Berlin office of David Chipperfield Architects for the restoration of the NCBRAS and surrounding buildings I was pleased to receive a letter from them requesting my assistance in early March 2009. I felt reassured that the fate of the building was in their good hands. I was even more reassured when they explained that 'our brief is to create an exhibition and events centre [...] so the building in its new role will maintain some

Figure 11 & 12: The NCBRAS Building before renovation in January 2008, and after renovation June 2010

connection with its history.'

Mark Randel, a director of the Berlin office took charge of the project on the ground. Apart from sharing my research and insights with Mark, I also shared my ambition for the Society to have some presence in the building again, Indeed, he earmarked a small space for our use in one iteration of his plans, which was sadly not approved. Despite that I felt a deep sense of pride when the building reopened as the Rockbund Art Museum (RAM) on 3 May 2010, with David Chipperfield himself present, in the knowledge that the former president Sowerby's dream for a modern art gallery to be installed in the building finally took place, 55 years after his passing.

I was delighted in being able to tell of Sowerby's engagement in the building in a substantive article published in the catalogue of the Time Traveler Exhibition, held at RAM from the end of October till mid-December 2012, where the historical narrative of the museum had been reinvented by artists as 'natural works of art'.[14] It was enormously satisfying to reflect on how the fortunes of Society's past and present, represented by Sowerby in the early 20th century, and myself a century later, had coalesced in the same place. I left Shanghai, some six months after this event, in the knowledge that the RAS had successfully reinstated itself as an important part of life in Shanghai for so many people.

Thanks for the Memory of two wonderfully passionate dear friends, Pixie Gray and Michelle Blumenthal, who lived and loved life to the full.

DISCLAIMER *This article draws upon some of my previously published works as well primary sources including old emails and extensive RAS records of the Society's meetings and activities, as well as upon my fragile memory. I extend my apologies for any inaccuracies or glaring omissions contained herein. References to the history of the Hangzhou Branch and direct quotes are taken from Dr. Judith Kolbas' upcoming 200*th *anniversary retrospective of the establishment of the society in Hangzhou for the RAS London journal.*

PETER HIBBARD *was a visiting scholar at the Centre of Asian Studies, Hong Kong University in 1985/86. He subsequently lectured at the Beijing Institute of Tourism and travelled overland to every province and region of China by 1990. From 1991, Peter worked as a China tour director and a Shanghai raconteur. His lifetime research on the history of tourism in China and Shanghai's urban development resulted in many publications, including Bund Shanghai: China Faces West, and Peace at the Cathay. He returned from Shanghai to England in 2013, but is proud to be an honorary Vice-president of RAS China and occasionally returns to Hong Kong and the mainland in his role as Heritage and Archive Ambassador of The Peninsula hotel, Hong Kong.*

———◆◇◆———

REFERENCES

1 Hibbard, Peter, *The Bund Shanghai: China Faces West* (Hong Kong: Odyssey, 2007).
2 Royal Asiatic Society Hong Kong, History of the Royal Asiatic Society Hong Kong, https://www.royalasiaticsociety.org.hk/history [accessed on 6 June 2023].
3 *North China Herald*, 19 April 1933, p. 83.
4 NCBRAS Journal Vol. 58, 1927, *Proceedings* p. xii.
5 NCBRAS Journal, Vol. 70, 1941, *Proceedings*, page ii.
6 Fraser, Sir Everard, NCBRAS Journal Vol. 45, 1914, *Proceedings* p. vii.
7 Pringle, Henry F, *Bridge House Survivor: Experiences of a Civilian Prisoner-of-war in Shanghai & Beijing 1942–45* (Hong Kong: Earnshaw Books, 2010).
8 Liu, Elizabeth Gill, *Open Hearts Open Doors: Reflections on China's*

Past and Present (Los Angeles: Cornell University Press, 2008).

9 de Carle Sowerby, Arthur, *China's Natural History: A Guide to the Shanghai Museum (R.A.S.)* (Shanghai, North China Branch of the Royal Asiatic Society, 1936).

10 Hibbard, Peter and Editors, Preface, *Journal of The Royal Asiatic Society China in Shanghai,* 74, 1.

11 Author's personal recollections.

12 Shen, Lindsay, *Knowledge is Pleasure: Florence Ayscough in Shanghai* (Hong Kong: Hong Kong University Press, 2012).

13 Witchard, Anne, *Lao She in London* (Hong Kong: Hong Kong University Press, 2012).

14 Hibbard, Peter, *More thàn a Stuffed Bird Show: The RAS Legacy in Shanghai,* (RAS Lecture Series, London: Royal Asiatic Society of Great Britain and Ireland, 23 October 2018).

SECTION 3

Lives Well Lived

CHINESE CHARACTER: ZHOU YOUGUANG, THE FATHER OF CHINA'S *PINYIN* SYSTEM

By Mark O'Neill

ABSTRACT

This is an article about The Man Who Made China a Literate Nation—a biography of Zhou Youguang, *published in English only by Joint Publishing of Hong Kong in the autumn of 2023. The article describes Zhou's extraordinary life of 111 years, as the father of Hanyu Pinyin, the system of writing Chinese characters with Romanised letters in use since 1958. More than one billion Chinese have learnt it. Zhou chose to return to the mainland in 1949 and lived through the campaigns of the Maoist period. He spent 28 months in a labour camp in Ningxia, west China. In addition, he wrote 49 books, many critical of the Soviet Union, the Soviet model used in China and of Mao Zedong. In the last 20 years of his life, he was one of the few intellectuals in China willing to speak the truth in public. He lived so long thanks to an innate optimism, intellectual curiosity about everything and a Buddhist-like humility to see himself and his belongings as of little value.*

When young children arrive in primary school in China, they first attend a Chinese language class where the teacher teaches them not Chinese characters but Pinyin, a romanization system using Roman letters with four different tones. Once they have mastered it, then the teacher starts to teach them characters; thanks to the Pinyin next to each character, they can read it. Without it, they would not know how to pronounce them. It is this system—full name Hanyu Pinyin (漢語拼音), meaning Chinese phonetics—which has turned China into a literate nation. It was introduced in 1958, when 80 per cent of the population was illiterate. Since then, a billion people have learnt Pinyin and the rate of illiteracy has fallen to below 10 per cent. In numbers of people it has made literate, it is the greatest achievement in linguistics in human history. The man most responsible for Pinyin is Zhou Youguang (周有光), director of the department in the Chinese Character Reform Commission (CCRC); in 1955, he was instructed to create a new romanisation system.

Zhou was one of the most remarkable Chinese intellectuals of the last two centuries. Born in January 1906, he lived under four 'dynasties'—the Qing, the Beiyang government, the Kuomintang and the Communists. He died on January 14, 2017, one day after his 111 birthday. He wrote a total of 49 books. In 1949, he was working in London as the representative of a Chinese bank. He agonised over whether or not to live in a China under Communist rule; in the end, he decided to return, and spent the remaining 69 years of his life there. He lived through all the tragedies of Maoist rule. He spent 28 months in a labour camp in the western region of Ningxia and returned to Beijing to find that Red Guards had removed every single item from his apartment—not one piece of paper or photograph remained. He went back to his office to be told that he and other intellectuals were the 'dregs of society' and had no value; they would be given a minimum salary to keep them alive for humanitarian reasons only. He endured these humiliations with a Buddhist-like humility; he attached little importance to himself or his work.

Throughout his life, he retained an intense curiosity about everything, earning the nickname "Encyclopaedia Zhou" (周百科), and a warmth and openness that won him many friends, Chinese and foreign. After his official retirement in 1991 at the age of 84, he turned out books and articles on a wide range of topics. He was one of the few Chinese intellectuals willing to criticise publicly the government of Mao Zedong and the Soviet model which Mao had followed. Since some books could not be published in the mainland, they were published instead in Hong Kong and Taiwan. His advanced age and high status as the "Father of Pinyin" saved him from arrest and prison and allowed him to meet a constant stream of visitors. On the last day of his life, he was due to meet American Dr Vinton Gray Cerf, one of the founders of the Internet. Cerf wanted to thank him for Pinyin, which had become one of the most important tools that Chinese use to access the net. Cerf was about to leave for Zhou's apartment when he heard the news of his passing. He made a plaque, written in English and Chinese: 'In memory of Zhou Youguang whose brilliant and persistent invention of Pinyin helped to bring the Internet and its applications within reach of the Chinese-speaking community.' I venture to say that, when Zhou arrived at the gates of Paradise, the angels opened the gates for him without the need of the interview or examination of documents required for the rest of us. Who else

130

among us has used their time on earth to such a good purpose?

He was fortunate to be born into an upper middle class and well-educated family in Changzhou, Jiangsu province, one of the most prosperous regions of China. He studied at primary and secondary schools in the city. The Changzhou Middle School was an all-male boarding establishment, where the standard of English was very high. World history, chemistry, geography and biology were all taught in English. Then, in 1923, he went on to St John's University in Shanghai, one of the top colleges in China. His family could not afford the fees, but a friend graciously stepped in and provided the money he needed. He chose economics as his major, with linguistics as an elective. The university used English as its medium of instruction. An excellent student, he appreciated the culture of his teachers—many of them foreigners—to promote a critical faculty among their students and give them only limited homework. Two years later, he was among 553 students who left St John's after it refused to allow them to join a citywide strike against the killing by British-led police of nine protestors in the May 30th Incident. They set up a new university, Kwang Hwa, from which he graduated two years later. On April 30, 1933, in Shanghai, he married Zhang Yunhe, the well-educated daughter of a wealthy Suzhou family. She went on to become one of China's leading experts on Kunqu Opera.

Their marriage was very happy and lasted more than 70 years. For his graduate studies, Zhou preferred the United States, but did not have the money. So he went to Japan, where he studied at Kyoto Imperial University and learned Japanese. After his return to Shanghai in 1935, he worked at the Bank of Jiangsu and taught economics at Kwang Hwa University.

For Zhou, like millions of Chinese, the war with Japan which started in 1937 was a Calvary. With his family, he escaped to Chongqing, the wartime capital. He became an official of the Agriculture Bureau, a unit of the Ministry of Economic Affairs, and was deputy commissioner for Sichuan province. Its mission was to feed and clothe the members of China's armed forces and the population under the control of the National Government. To avoid Japanese bombing, Zhou and his family moved 36 times. He narrowly escaped death on several occasions. In April 1942, in Jinhua, Zhejiang province, Zhou met James Doolittle, one of the most famous American pilots of World War II who had just led 16 bombers over

Tokyo in the first American bombing raid over the Japanese capital. After the raid, the pilots flew westward and landed or bailed out by parachute in China. Zhou served as interpreter between Doolittle and his fellow pilots and the Chinese officers hosting him. In 1946, when he was working in New York, Zhou visited Doolittle in his sumptuous office at the Shell Oil Company, where he was a vice-president. On his return to Chongqing, Zhou learnt of the loss of their six-year daughter to peritonitis; the medicine she had been taking in Shanghai was not available in Chongqing.

At the end of the war, the family returned to their home in Suzhou and found there was nothing left; during their eight-year absence, everything had been taken. Zhou went to work for the Xinhua Bank, which sent him to run its operation in New York. During his two years in the United States, Zhou seized every opportunity to learn and to meet Americans. He attended lectures and read until closing time at the New York Public Library. His job enabled him to meet managers and chief executives of large companies. He came to admire many things about Americans—their optimism, entrepreneurship and openness. He also admired the factors behind America's economic success—the intense competition between companies, the financial system, the railway system and the widespread use of shorthand. There was much China could learn. At Princeton University, he met Albert Einstein.

Then he spent a year in Britain, which was falling behind the USA as an industrial power. He found rationing and foreign exchange controls in place, even after the war. During 1949, his final year in London, he and his wife had to make an existential decision—whether to return to a China under Communist control? Thanks to three years of working abroad, he had foreign exchange savings enough to start a new life in the USA. He was fluent in English and had a network of contacts and experience in business and teaching that would have brought a comfortable life in the USA. His American friends told him not to return. But his Chinese friends had a different opinion. They said that life in the USA would be comfortable but without meaning. Since it was already a developed country, what contribution could he make as a foreigner? The USA had a deep well of talent and Chinese had no say in politics. After 12 years of war and destruction, China had so much rebuilding to do, and qualified people like Zhou could make an important contribution. In the end, he decided to return. His family and that of his wife lived in China; they had sent their son to school in Suzhou, not Manhattan. Like many intellectuals, he detested the Kuomintang and believed the promises of the Communist leaders to introduce democracy, freedom of assembly, opinion, organisation, publication, to strike and organise opposition parties.

Back in Shanghai in late 1949, Zhou continued to work at Xinhua Bank and lectured in economics at Fudan University. Then things began to change dramatically, more rapidly than Zhou had imagined. The new government nationalised all the banks and merged more than 20 faculties of economics. He continued to teach; but, like his colleagues, he had to throw away his materials and teach only translations of Soviet textbooks. His students asked him to explain Keynesian Economics, but he did not dare. He had no time for Soviet 'economics'. In 1951, the first campaign began; some staff of the banks were so frightened that they took their own lives by jumping out of their offices on the Bund. Working for the People's Educational Publishing Company, Zhou's wife was labelled 'a big tiger' and had to write a 'confession' of 20,000 characters; it was not accepted. She was traumatised, her weight fell to 40 kilograms and her teeth fell out. She returned to live with Zhou in Shanghai. Finally, the investigation found nothing against her. The trauma was so profound that she and Zhou decided that she would never return to full-time work again. 'If I had been working during the Cultural Revolution, I would certainly have died,' she said.

In 1955, Zhou's life was transformed. The government moved him from Shanghai to Beijing to the Chinese Character Reform Commission (CCRC), where he would work for the rest of his life. He had published two books on how to use the Roman alphabet to write Chinese. Mao Zedong read the second, *The Subject of the Alphabets* published in November 1954. It persuaded him to accept a phonetic system based on the Roman alphabet, rather than one using strokes of the characters or the Cyrillic alphabet. It was a momentous decision. The move saved Zhou from prison and possibly worse. During the anti-rightist campaign of 1957, professors of economics in Shanghai were a prime target, especially those who had studied or worked in 'imperialist' countries. If he had still been in Shanghai, he would have been sent to prison or labour camp; some professors took their own lives.

At the CCRC, Zhou was put in charge of the division responsible for creating a phonetic system. He threw himself with his customary energy into understanding the different systems used around the world.

It took him and his team three years of intense work. They were subject to sharp criticism; some said pinyin should not be based on the Roman alphabet and that he was "a slave of the West." He and the team created an alphabet as close as possible to the sound of the characters; they added to each character one of the four tones in Mandarin. In 1958, Mao gave his approval. Then Pinyin was formally approved by the CCRC and then the National People's Congress. He and the government began to spread the new system across China, especially in the schools. It remains in use today.

Zhou was invited to join the Chinese People's Political Consultative Congress (CPPCC), the top advisory body to the government. He served in it for more than 20 years until he resigned in protest after the military crackdown in June 1989. Through his participation, Zhou met national leaders including Mao, Zhou Enlai and Deng Xiaoping. He watched helpless as the party implemented one campaign after another—the Anti-Rightist Campaign, the Great Leap Forward and the Cultural Revolution. In the first, his new position in the CCRC and as a specialist in linguistics—politically neutral—saved him from persecution; but many of his friends were affected, sometimes with tragic results. On the Great Leap Forward, he later said in an interview: 'it led to the death of tens of millions of farmers and a very sharp fall in output of grain. The people had nothing to eat … In recent years, I read foreign materials which gave a conservative estimate of 45 million dead from starvation. It was the biggest disaster in the history of China.'

But he did not escape during the Cultural Revolution. He was labeled a "counter-revolutionary academic authority" (反動學術權威) and had to live in a "cow pen" for such undesirables in a garage of the CRCC. He and his wife had to dispose of their many books and destroy many precious photographs. In November 1969, he and other "bad elements" were sent to a labour camp in Ningxia, west China. 'We had to swear an oath that we would never return to our original homes,' Zhou said later. 'In fact, it was an oath to say that society did not need people like us. We were the dregs of society. This was the Soviet model. The Soviet Union sent old intellectuals, capitalists and landowners to places north of the Arctic Circle.' They did farm labour, self-evaluation and studied the works of Mao Zedong. One assignment was to guard the sorghum harvested by the camp with another inmate. This turned out to be Lin Handa (林漢達). With a Ph.D. in education from Colorado University, he was Vice-Minister of Education in the 1950s; in 1958, he was declared a "rightist" and, during the Cultural Revolution a "counter-revolutionary".

How did Zhou survive this ordeal? He said later: 'The Cadre School was very interesting. I turned a bad thing into something enjoyable. I was an optimist and never lost hope. I believed that every bad thing would finally become a good thing.'

It was this spirit that enabled him to live until 111 and achieve so much in his life. In the spring of 1972, he finally returned to Beijing, having spent 28 months in Ningxia. When he and his wife entered their apartment, they found that the Red Guards had stripped it of everything—books, articles, notes and photographs. This was the second time in their life that they had lost everything. He was remarkably calm. 'During the Sino-Japanese war, there was death and escape,' he said. 'Compared to the suffering of that war, the Cultural Revolution was a minor matter. I had no attachment to the items in our house. This attitude was a big help. Our feeling toward assets was very shallow. We felt that it was something outside the body. There is a saying in Buddhism: "If you regard items outside the body as important, your spirit will suffer pain"'.

After the Cultural Revolution, one of his jobs at the CCRC was to receive foreign guests. At that time, not many people in China had his foreign language and social skills. His guests gave him gifts; he never took them home but left them in the official car for the driver to give to his family.

But his verdict on the Cultural Revolution was scathing. He said that it continued for several years after Mao's death, and no fundamental changes until the early 1980s. 'So it actually lasted for 15 years. What was the purpose of this catastrophe? I do not understand.' One of the thousands of deaths during the Cultural Revolution was that of Liu Shaoqi, Chairman of State between 1959 and 1968. He died on the morning of November 12, 1969 while living under an assumed name in Kaifeng, Henan province. 'Liu's death was very tragic. It is said that, when he died, he was naked. His body was wrapped in a mat and thrown into a crematorium without a name … I do not understand. Why was there destruction on such a large scale? The whole education system was shut down for 10 years, influencing an entire generation of people. The Cultural Revolution caused a loss of trust in the Communist Party. This crisis of trust was very frightening. In the early 1950s, the country's political system was stable and the government was methodical. Under the leadership of Zhou Enlai, people had trust in the government. But one movement after another destroyed this trust—including the anti-rightist movement and the People's Communes.' The concentration of power in the hands of one man, Chairman Mao, he said, was like that of many emperors in Chinese history. 'So some people said that Chairman Mao achieved two formidable things in his life. One was to create New China. The other was to destroy it.'

Pinyin gradually became the international standard for written Chinese. In 1982, the International Organization for Standardization (ISO) adopted it, with the number ISO-7098. In 1986, the United Nations adopted Pinyin. Singapore adopted Pinyin for teaching Chinese in its schools, shortly after launching its Speak Mandarin Campaign in 1979. In the USA, agencies of the Federal Government, the scholarly community and the media adopted Pinyin. On October 1, 2000, the USA Library of Congress started to use it.

Between 1980 and 1985, Zhou left China several times, to visit Hong Kong, Hawaii and the United States. Between October 1984 and February 1985, he spent four months in the USA, travelling from California through the Midwest to New York. Famous as the scholar who had created Pinyin, he was in great demand as a lecturer; he spoke at universities in Santa Barbara and Yale and at the United Nations. During this period, his main project was as one of three editors charged with translating 10 volumes of the Encyclopedia Britannica into Chinese. The first Chinese version was published in 1985, in 10 volumes, with more than 7000 topics, 5000 maps and a total of 24 million characters. Since then, the Chinese version has continued to expand, reaching 20 volumes in 2007. Zhou was an ideal person for this project. Interested in everything, he had a broad knowledge of many subjects, in addition to his specialties of economics and linguistics.

The greatest contribution of Pinyin has been to enable tens of millions of Chinese to become literate in their own language, as well as to help millions of foreigners to learn it. It has also played a major role in taking Chinese into the electronic age and turning it into the second most used language on the Internet, after English. This is something beyond the imagination of Hu Shih, Chao Yuen-ren and other language reformers of the early decades of the 20th century. With the rapid improvements in technology, there are today many ways to input Chinese into a computer, including voice recognition. Pinyin remains one of the most popular, for both Chinese and non-Chinese.

At the end of 1991, Zhou officially retired, two weeks before his 85th birthday. At that age, most people would have chosen a life of long lunches, chess, card and mahjong games with their family and friends, tourism, reading novels and naps after lunch. But Zhou did the opposite. During his remaining 26 years, he wrote more than 20 books; he averaged one article a month and one book every three years, published on the mainland, Hong Kong and Taiwan. They covered a wide range of subjects, including history, literature, anthropology and poetry as well as his specialties of linguistics and economics. He lectured at Beijing and People's Universities. As he grew older, he became increasingly critical of the Communist Party, the Soviet model it had adopted, its version of history and its treatment of intellectuals like him. These subjects could not be addressed in publications in the mainland. But the authorities left him alone, probably because of his high status and advanced age. He said in an interview in April 2010: 'When you are young, you are naïve and follow blindly. In old age, you start to explore the truth. I am 105 and could die tomorrow. It is no problem to say the wrong thing. Others who write articles must be careful.' Another thing that sustained him was a constant stream of family, friends and visitors, Chinese and foreign. He was delighted to see them and exchange news and opinions. They marveled at his smile, jokes, optimism, stamina, encyclopedic knowledge and willingness to speak the truth. Foreign journalists sought him out for this reason. He was one of the few people in Beijing willing to say publicly that the Emperor had no clothes.

How did he live so long? He did not drink or smoke, nor eat health supplements. 'Do not get angry. Be more tolerant,' he said. 'I am an optimist. Whatever difficulties you face, see the good aspect. The bad aspects will slowly pass … My best tonic is remaining curious and continuing to learn.' He was also sustained by humility and contentment with a simple life. 'My life is very ordinary, with no special value. I am an average person … God is too busy and has forgotten me.' When visitors praised him as "the Father of Pinyin", he would modestly answer that he was "the Son of Pinyin" or one of its main creators. 'It is the result of a long tradition from the later years of the Qing dynasty down to today. But we restudied the problem, revisited it and made it more perfect.'

On 14 August 2002, he lost his beloved wife, at the age of 93. They had been married for 70 years. 'At 93, we should say that death is normal. Her passing was a bolt from the blue. I had never imagined one day when we would not be together. Such a blow suffocated me, but I had no alternative but to accept the law of nature … I thought that, since I was four years older than she, I would go sooner.' On 22 January 2015, his son, Zhou Xiaoping, a meteorologist, died, at the age of 80.

Zhou passed away on 14 January 2017, one day after his 111th birthday. His funeral was held on January 19 at a funeral home in an eastern suburb of Beijing, attended by family members and many friends. His passing provoked an outpouring of grief. 'You were my dear friend for decades,' wrote Victor Mair, Professor of Chinese at the University of Pennsylvania. 'I wish that you had gone on living forever. You will be sorely missed, but yours was a life well lived. As the "Father of Pinyin", you have had an enormous impact on education and culture in China. After you passed the century mark, you spoke out courageously in favor of democracy and reform. Now, one day after your 111th birthday, you have departed, but you will always be in our hearts, brimming with light, as your name suggests'.

Mark O'Neill (www.mark-0neill.com) has lived in Asia since 1978. He has written 14 books on Chinese history and society. Of these, eight have editions in Chinese as well as English. He was inspired to write a biography of Zhou Youguang due to Zhou's great contribution to humanity, in common with the subjects of O'Neill's other biographies— his grandfather, an Irish Presbyterian missionary in Manchuria from 1897 to 1942; Sir Robert Hart, Director-General of the Imperial Maritime Customs from 1863 to 1911; and Dr Hu Shih, who was, like Zhou, one of China's great intellectuals of the 20th century. Born in London, England, O'Neill was educated at Marlborough College and New College, Oxford and worked in Washington D.C., Manchester and Belfast before moving to Asia.

BIBLIOGRAPHY Zhou Youguang's oral autobiography *My Hundred Years as I Told It* 周有光百年口述，我所度過的時光，Chinese University of Hong Kong Press, 2015

Chen Guangzhong, *Follow and Read Zhou Youguang* 走讀周有光，陳光中，華品文創出版社，臺北，November 2012, Chinese Creation Publishing Co, Taipei, November 2012

A DIPLOMATIC MERCHANT IN CHINA: HERMAN W. BREUER

By Christine Maiwald

ABSTRACT

Herman W. Breuer was a merchant in Shanghai from 1906 to 1952, whose lifelong interaction with China included several distinct periods. From 1906 to 1945, he was working for a German import-export firm. He became chairman of the German Community Shanghai from 1949 to 1952 and, as such, quasi-Consul. Back in Germany in 1952 at the age of 70, he worked as a government employee assessing German property lost in East Asia and was chairman of the East Asian Association in Bremen. Using a comprehensive archive of family letters, his great niece reconstructs significant events of his life in China and Germany.

INTRODUCTION

Reflecting on the nature of historical development, the eminent German historian and sinologist, Mechthild Leutner, Professor of Society, State, and Culture of Modern China, observed,

> [H]istory—here the history of German-Chinese relations—does not develop as it were, within economic conditions and political structures, nor is it shaped, promoted or hindered by individual well-known great personalities [...], but that this promotion or hindrance of history is always shaped by a number of people within certain contexts. History is a collective work, a collective action, even if it is often only attributed to certain individuals, the respective personalities of the group of main stakeholders.[1]

Introducing her biographical sketch of the German diplomat Dr Erich Michelsen, Prof. Leutner goes on,

> This is the story of a personality who has only received marginal attention in historical research, who has been, on a middle level, actively involved in shaping German-

Chinese relations in practice for more than three decades and whose contribution to these relations has so far hardly been mentioned.

(Translation by author)

It is such a life 'on a middle level' that is the subject of this article: Hermann W. Breuer (1884 to 1973) a German merchant in China (Shanghai from 1906 to 1952), accepted diplomatic functions thrust upon him in a difficult time (1949 to 1952), turned government employee and consultant when he was almost 70 (1953 to 1963), and, as the chairman of the East-Asian Association in Bremen, kept politicians, diplomats and merchants informed about China until his death, at almost 90 years old. His life was, almost from the start, closely entwined with German-Chinese history and the international community in Shanghai. Following his version of a Rotarian motto 'that sensible charity and practical help are a good foundation for human society',[2] he supported his compatriots as well as Chinese and international friends in adversity.

Hermann W. Breuer was born in Bangkok, where his father Oskar Breuer was secretary at the German Consulate. During his early childhood he lived in Hong Kong and Sumatra. At the age of six, Hermann was sent to school in Hanover, Germany. After a commercial apprenticeship with the *Allgemeine Elektricitäts-Gesellschaft* (General Electricity Company AEG, founded 1883) he did one year's military service.

Hermann Breuer was a godson of Hermann Melchers, founder of Melchers & Co., China, the Asian branch of the Bremen merchants C. Melchers & Co. The Shanghai venture, set up in 1877, had been the second branch of Melchers in China after Hong Kong (1866), and was followed by further branches. They were not only an import-export firm they also processed certain goods (e.g. dried egg white and yolk, soya bean oil and wine), they were insurance agents and the sole Asian agent of North German Lloyd.[3]

SOCIAL LIFE AND THE FIRST WORLD WAR

In the summer of 1906, Hermann Melchers sent Breuer to Shanghai, where he started work as a junior clerk, at a time when China was embarking on exchanges with Western commerce and banking. The Self-Strengthening Movement and Qing reforms used Western imports and loans. Germany's trade with China began to flourish.

In addition to fulfilling his office duties, Breuer took part in the typical sporting and social life of Europeans in Shanghai at the time. He joined the German Company of the Shanghai Volunteer Corps (he proved to be a "crack shot"), the fire-fighters, and the rowing club. He went house-boating, hunting and dancing, played tennis and was a dedicated horseman. He became a member of the German Club

Figure 1: Breuer in the office of Melchers & Co. in Shanghai around 1906.

Concordia and a shareholder in the German Garden Club. But most important for him was that, in business and also privately, he was getting to know the 'gigantic Chinese empire.'[4]

In 1913, during his first home leave, Hermann Breuer married Erna Wolcke from Hamburg whom he had courted when she was visiting relatives in Shanghai. During the Great War only the less experienced Melchers' staff were released from their contracts in order to take up arms and defend the German concession Qingdao against the Japanese. Breuer, at the age of 30, had to stay in Shanghai, where he was among the first to support the Qingdao relief fund. As business slowed down considerably during the war and social life came to a standstill, Breuer intensified his studies of Mandarin, mastering more than 1200 Chinese characters.

After the first year of the war, the international treaty port spirit of Shanghai dissolved into nationalisms; Germans became outcasts. When China joined the war on the side of the Entente in 1917, German property was confiscated and accounts with the German Asiatic Bank (DAB) rationed.[5] In 1919 the bank was dissolved. In March and early April 1919, while the Versailles peace treaty was being negotiated, Germans were repatriated. Breuer was among the very few who were allowed to stay (for a limited time), because his wife was pregnant. Their son Uwe was born in June.

Breuer was able, with the help of Chinese business contacts, to get some of Melchers' business going again. In September 1919 China declared peace with Germany and, in early 1920 revoked the trade embargo. The Melchers team was at the ready, partner Adolf Widmann having returned to Shanghai. Supported by Chinese partners, Chinese banks and former compradors, Melchers could start again, as did other German firms. Additionally, in 1921 Melchers acquired an American "cloak" to further international trading under the name *Melchers China Corporation* and Breuer was invested with power of attorney. Having restarted from a garret on Broadway (Dongdaming Lu), the firm moved into a palatial building on 10—11 Jiujiang Road in 1924.[6]

The building housed offices for the diverse Melchers departments: shipping, insurance, export and Breuer's import department with fifteen European and twenty-five to thirty Chinese staff.[7] There were showrooms which the import department had furnished with an exhibition of prototype merchandise, presenting textiles, papers, clocks and watches, optical instruments, hurricane lamps, stoves, kettles, wash jugs and bowls, thermos flasks, perfume and soap, and hardware (ironmongery): knives, fittings, locks and bolts.

In the early 1920s, Melchers' imports to China benefited from the inflation in Germany; merchandise was cheap in spite of the relatively

Figure 2: Melchers' hong on the French Bund, circa 1900.

high customs duties on German goods (in the 1921 peace and trade treaty with China, Germany had lost the position of "privileged nation").

As Breuer gained trust and recognition in his working life, his marriage began to break down. His wife Erna now lived openly as a lesbian. She returned to Germany with their son in early 1921. When Breuer was on furlough in 1922, the couple tried to find a new understanding, but she did not go back with him to Shanghai and as soon as Breuer was in China, friends informed him that she was again living with her female friend. His sad conclusion was: 'The loving partner is hit hard and bitterly by the experience.'[8]

From 1924, Breuer became a member of various boards: When on the 12th of December 1924 the Paper Importers Association was established, he was elected to the committee; from 1932 he would serve as vice-president.[9] The Association represented approximately twenty-five European firms. During the first Annual General Meeting it was said that

> [...] both foreign importers and Chinese dealers agreed that the Association, by introducing new terms of sale, has eliminated the speculative elements [...] and has placed the paper business on a sound footing.[10]

From 1930, annual reports would reflect the general trade depression, with the paper importers also striving against Japanese competition. Even at times when the depression was deeply felt, the paper trade was better off than other dealers because of the backing the Association could give.[11]

In addition to the more positive business environment, social activities began to flourish again. The year 1925 saw the re-emergence of the German Amateur Dramatic Club (*Deutscher Theater-Verein*—ADC)[12] and Breuer was elected as its president. He had no artistic ambitions, neither as an amateur actor nor as a director, but he brought his longstanding contacts with German and foreign merchants, and his diplomatic and financial skills to the honorary job. This was crucial at the time because the German ADC was part of the resurrection of the German community in Shanghai after the war: it was to be its showcase. From the opening of the 1925/26 season, the German players were again invited to use the English Lyceum

Theatre[13], and were also allowed to play in the Carlton Theatre, the American Players' venue; they could borrow costumes and decorations of English productions. Early copies of the journal *Bühnenspiegel im Fernen Osten* are full of thanks to those clubs for their cooperation. This was induced by genuine gratitude but it also drew attention to the fact that the other European nations were willing to let Germans play again on the international stage in China.

In 1926, Breuer accepted his election to the arbitration board of the German Residents' Association. Also in 1926, Melchers reverted to open German ownership (*Melchers & Co., China*) and Breuer became head of the import department and pay partner, i.e. the only employee who, in addition to the full partners, was authorised to "sign for the firm".[14] He went on one of his long journeys north, visiting Melchers' branches in Qingdao and Tianjin, and business partners in Beijing, Shenyang and Dalian with a last stop at Melchers Hankou (Wuhan). Imports again comprised everything from needles and nails to motor bikes and cars. In addition, the company was involved in large business ventures like the construction of the Zhabei power plant[15] in the late 1920s, and of a radio station, which opened in Shanghai in December 1930.[16]

Figure 3: Melchers' office building on Jiujiang Lu, 1924 to 1945.

When Melchers decided to re-establish a branch in Qingdao (before the Great War, they had had a *hong,* or trading house, in the harbour area),[17] Breuer was entrusted with overseeing the new venture from Shanghai. In 1926, they started from scratch in a small office within the newly built stock exchange. In Qingdao, Melchers also undertook other commercial enterprises, bottling *Iltis*—water from springs in the Laoshan Mountains, producing lemonade and the *Melco* vermouth.[18] New offices in Kwan Hsien Road, also for the agency of North German Lloyd, were opened in 1929. Whenever he was in Qingdao, Breuer went on hiking tours in the Laoshan Mountains and he also visited the seaside resort Beidaihe. Other trips took him to the mountain resorts Moganshan and Guling and the sulphur springs in Unzen, Japan—never forgetting to send postcards to family members in Germany.

The year 1929 saw the opening of Melchers' state of the art godown on Shanghai's Broadway (Dongdaming Lu) near Chaufoong Road (Gaoyang Lu), next to the Shanghai & Hongkew Wharf. As the warehouse was partly built for storing imported goods, Breuer, in his capacity as head of the department, had been consulted as to the requirements of the new building, which was also used for sorting and controlling goods (like tobacco and rhubarb) prior to export. Passengers' luggage and goods to be conveyed by North German Lloyd were put in storage there. The warehouse had a sixty-five meters wide front facing the Huangpu. Built of reinforced concrete, its six storeys were fitted with the latest technical equipment, like modern fire protection, an electric lift and a wide ramp up to the roof. The festive opening ceremony was presided over by Melchers China Partner, Adolf Widmann, with addresses by the acting German Consul General Dr Bracklo, and by the Chairman of the German Chamber of Commerce, and attended by the architect Emil Busch, guests from the business community, compradors, partners and employees. The *China Press* mentioned that 'The original site of Melchers & Co., comprising of offices and godowns, was on the French Bund, but in 1917 it was confiscated by the French authorities and sold.'[19]

The 23rd of July 1931, in a time of world economic crisis, saw the twenty-fifth anniversary of Breuer's life in China, and with Melchers & Co. Melchers' partner, Dr Adalbert Korff, recognised the prominent part Breuer had played in the reconstruction of Melchers' import business, in a ceremony honouring his contribution. Korff described how Breuer's decades of working closely with Chinese compatriots had generated 'a deep sympathy and love for his "second fatherland"'. Breuer was proud that many of his Chinese friends and delegates from the diverse merchant families and guilds came to congratulate him on his day of honour. The speaker for the Chinese business community was W. T. Liu, president of the Guild of Woollen Yarn and owner of the Shing Shing Tai Mill; while the venerable P.C. Loh spoke on behalf of Melchers' Chinese staff.[20]

In 1936 Breuer was due for another home leave. He went by the SS *Potsdam*, one of three newly built passenger liners on North German Lloyd's Far Eastern route (his way back would take place on her sister ship, the SS *Scharnhorst*). These comfortably equipped ships shortened the journey between Bremen and Shanghai from 52 to 34 days.[21]

He visited Melchers in Bremen and also many business contacts, among them A. Wulfing & Co. in Amsterdam. Melchers represented Wulfing & Co.'s restoratives, for instance *Sanatogen,* which promised the ever-ailing Shanghai population 'New Energy And Better Health'.[22] He also visited the Leipzig Trade Fair and DKW (DampfKraftWagen - Steam Power Car) in Zschopau, Saxony.[23] DKW produced motorcycles, motorcars, trucks and three-wheeled lorries, for which Melchers was sole importer in China. While in Saxony, he would have looked up the firm Hermann Nier in Beierfeld. Their oil-lamps (hurricane lamps) had for years been a staple of Melchers' imports to China. The majority had gone via Tianjin to Manchuria where trade was now in great danger of being appropriated by the Japanese following their occupation of the Chinese province in 1932. In spite of trade contracts with Germany they would, in 1938, forbid the import of German oil lamps into Manchuria.[24]

THE SHADOW OF A NEW WAR

This visit was also Breuer's first exposure to Fascism in Germany. There were serious consultations with his brother Karl who had invented a story explaining why the siblings did not have any proof of their mother's lineage. Karl had managed to hide the fact that their mother had been of Jewish descent which meant that according to the Nuremberg Laws her children were "first degree crossbreeds" (*Mischlinge ersten Grades*)[25]. As such they would be denied full citizenship rights and suffer from economic and social isolation—not only in Germany, but also in the

German business community of Shanghai.

Breuer was an open-minded liberal; it was obvious that he was no friend of the Nazis. Early on, he had been accused of not attending a single Nazi event in Shanghai—a colleague had spied on him and denounced him. In spite of his own precarious situation and in spite of an official interdiction, he gave work to German and Austrian Jewish refugees who had fled to Shanghai, where they did not need a visa, as a port of last resort.[26]

Figure 4: Breuer in the 1930s.

In August 1937, the undeclared Chinese–Japanese war came to Shanghai. Japanese soldiers did not enter the foreign settlements, but war was all around; misdirected bombs did terrible damage and cost thousands of lives. By the end of October the Japanese had seized the Chinese parts of Shanghai; the foreign settlements had become enclaves. Those were now inundated with refugees, mostly Chinese. Breuer was hosting a 50-year-old German woman who had fled from a Japanese occupied zone where she had lost everything. She tried to commit suicide while staying with him, but she was saved from self harm.

In the occupied areas, Chinese property was being expropriated. The Japanese also tried to seize the Wing On Textile Company's Factory No. 1 and the Dah Twa Dyeing Factory in the Eastern district Yangtzepu. In 1946, in a report to the Enemy Property Affairs Commission, a representative of the Wing On Textile Company explained the Japanese tactics:

> [They] used every means by either persuasion or threat to buy over, or to get a hand in the working of, these factories. The only way to reject the Japanese demands, and thereby save these properties, was, it appeared then, to get help from the Germans. So in Dec. 1937, we negotiated with

the German firm Melchers & Co. and succeeded in selling, nominally, the said two factories, including machinery, buildings, and land, to them. Agreements were formally signed, and Melchers & Co. rendered their help without asking for any compensation. In the following years, Melchers & Co. did their utmost in repulsing efforts of the Japanese to take these factories by repeated negotiations with the Japanese Foreign Ministry and the German Embassy in Shanghai. […] Therefore these two factories were practically saved by the help of Melchers & Co.[27]

In the winter of 1942, the Japanese released the military control of these two factories and the Wing On Textile Company was able to resume operation of them, but for the intervening five years, Breuer had acted as an unpaid manager for Wing On.

In 1939, Breuer was put in charge of Melchers' "special projects" which he reported to his family that he could not disclose in detail.[28] As their financial advisor, one of his tasks would become securing Melchers' earnings in times of war, which mainly meant buying real estate. Creating business opportunities in adverse circumstances had also been the driving-force behind Breuer's and Carl Gerhard Melchers' trips to the USA and return visits by representatives of their business partner the American Far Eastern Syndicate.[29]

The Second World War finally came to Shanghai on the 8th of December 1941, with Japan invading the International Settlement. When, from 1943, the Japanese interned non-combatant subjects of the allied nations, Breuer managed to assist internees, sending parcels of food and supplies. At the same time, his support found its way into the ghetto-like Hongkou area where, also from 1943, "stateless refugees" (meaning Jewish emigrants from Germany and occupied countries) were forced to live. In an anonymous letter to the editor the British sender gratefully remembers:

During the war, there were a few courageous Germans who, even when Hitler was winning, did not hesitate to denounce him […]. Such a one was Hermann Breuer. On more than one occasion he was threatened by the Gestapo; he was warned by the then very powerful German Consular Authorities, but in spite of this he continued to say what he thought, and, what is more, he continued to do all that a private individual could to help his allied friends. I for one will not forget his help and kindness during the dark days of the occupation. As well as helping British and American nationals, Hermann Breuer together with the Pastor of the German Church publicly organised help and relief for the German Jews concentrated in the Hongkou Ghetto. For this [...] Mr. Breuer faced the ostracism of many of his own nationals'.[30]

After the end of the war in Europe, in May 1945, the German community in Shanghai was in need of representatives unencumbered by a Nazi past. The Association of Free Germans, founded in August 1945, handed a list of 120 names of Germans to be classified as active anti-Nazis, among them Hermann Breuer, to the American secret service (OSS).[31] Breuer became a member of the 'German Emergency Office', active between mid-May and August. Being responsible for the Department of Social Affairs he had an emergency kitchen installed in the grounds of the German school (at the corner of Xan'an Xilu and Huashan Lu) where up to 500 Germans could get a warm meal each day. This earned him the nickname 'emergency cook'.[32] The kitchen was shut down when the East-Asian war ended and the Americans came to Shanghai and confiscated the school building and grounds. The remaining supplies were given to those Germans who were being interned in Lunghwa camp from October 1945 until deportation to Germany in August 1946. These were mostly diplomats and party officials, but also rank-and-file party members[33] and others to make up numbers preordained by the US military services.[34] Among those was the poet and journalist Hans Oberländer, a refugee for reasons of conscience whom Breuer had occasionally wined and dined.[35] In June 1945 Breuer was nominated supervisor for the elections to the new board of the German Residents' Association that was to succeed the board nominated by the Fascists. The anti-Nazi taipan Fred Siemssen was elected as new head of the board.[36]

By the end of September 1945, Melchers' property was confiscated and the old trading and shipping company had to declare the cessation of business. Breuer got a contract with Tai On, an offshoot of Wing On, who were longstanding business partners and Chinese friends of Melchers' and Breuer's, as their advisor on overseas affairs.

At that time, in the beginning of 1946, preparations had started for the repatriation of German nationals. In August, the first ship, the *Marine Robin*, carried about 1200 Germans home, predominantly Nazis, but also men of economic influence.[37] Breuer's name appeared on each of the three deportation lists compiled under American influence in 1946 and 1947. In August 1947 he was interned twice for imminent deportation, but Chinese friends in high places kept intervening on his behalf. At the very last minute they succeeded.

THE UNOFFICIAL DIPLOMAT

Breuer did not intend to go back to Germany. He had his job at Tai On that paid for his upkeep and enabled him to support his extended family and friends in Germany—he regularly sent food parcels, clothing and even little treats. Also, he was still living at a beautiful flat in the West Garden Mansions, Yu Yuan Lu (although a German couple had been billeted with him in 1945 when houses and apartments of Germans were requisitioned by Chinese citizens and American soldiers).[38]

Since moving into the flat in 1938, he had always shared it with his partner Jennie Bohanova and their two Gordon Setters. Jennie had come into his life some time after his divorce in 1926. She was born in Krasnoyarsk, Siberia in 1903 and, in 1921, had fled from the civil war in Russia to Harbin in north-eastern China. A beautiful petite woman 19 years Breuer's junior, she was a keen horsewoman and tennis player, loved dogs, dancing, flowers and cooking. She was tough and fun. In 1949, when it became obvious that the People's Liberation Army (PLA) was going to take over in China, she decided to flee once more and in April left Shanghai to join her brother in Sydney, Australia. When, in 1951, Breuer finally decided that he would return to Germany, Jennie did not consider accompanying him, because of the political situation there. The shock of the Berlin Blockade (June 1949—May 1949) still lingered. Jennie went to Los Angeles. They never met again.[39]

While Jennie was preparing to leave Shanghai, Hermann was elected Chairman of the German Residents' Association Shanghai. He was installed on the 15th of May, a few days before the PLA's conquest of the city on the 25th of May.[40] On the 26th Breuer telegraphed the East-Asian Association (*Ostasiatischer Verein*, OAV) in Hamburg informing them that the political takeover had been achieved without major unrest and that the seven hundred Germans still living in Shanghai were fine.[41] After a meeting with the Ministry of Foreign Affairs (the Wai Jiao Bu), the communists accepted him as Consul by default, as there was no alternative. He was instructed that he would be made personally responsible for the behaviour of every German living in China.[42]

Many companies had shut down shortly before the PLA reached Shanghai. Chinese taipans had fled to Taiwan and Hong Kong, Europeans also fled to Hong Kong or further. After Mao Zedong had proclaimed the Peoples' Republic of China and the PLA had established governance over all of mainland China, job opportunities for Europeans were ever more limited; property taxes were high and kept rising. As the financial pressures on Westerners in China resulted in disposition and forced emigration, many Germans were no longer able to pay for their journey home. In lieu of a diplomatic representation of West Germans in China (the Embassy of the GDR did not represent Germans in China at the time, since they were presumed "West Germans")[43], it became the task of the German Residents' Association in Shanghai, still the largest German community in China, to cooperate with the OAV in Hamburg, the shipping company Jebsen & Jessen in Hong Kong and, secretly, with administrative bodies in what had been Germany (which had become the "Bizone", then the "Trizone" and, from May 1949, the Federal Republic of Germany), in bringing destitute Germans home.[44]

In the second half of 1949, nearly one hundred destitute Germans from Harbin were taken on board the IRO (International Refugee Organisation) ship *Anna Salen* in Tianjin (generally, the IRO did not help Germans because they were not technically refugees). In November 1950, after one and a half years of negotiations, German-British cooperation succeeded in sending the ship *Dundalk Bay* to Tianjin, as the harbour of Shanghai was blocked by Kuomintang mines. But only about three hundred and fifty Germans embarked when seven hundred had been anticipated.[45] Some could not get exit permits, some wanted to guard property in China and some believed they would find work in China after all.

However, the Chinese intervention in the Korean War had started in mid-October of that year, and the situation for Westerners worsened considerably. When the propaganda campaign *Resist America, Aid Korea* was launched, widespread suspicion of espionage resulted in many arrests.[46] From then on, Breuer and his team organised individual transport for small groups whenever they were issued exit permits. The route went by rail from Shanghai to Hong Kong—or on ships from Tianjin—and on to Italy. From 1952, most transfers went by air from Hong Kong to Germany.

Breuer and the German Association had to argue the necessity of each return—and why people had not gone earlier. They described tragic fates and hopeless states of health. Breuer also had to decide on citizenship in cases of doubt (e.g. with cross-cultural marriages, surviving dependents, foster children). He had to decide who was allowed to travel, who got a cabin, who got sick treatment. The three or four people at his office were endlessly writing and amending lists with names and other data. Repatriation was more or less completed by the end of 1952; and the office was shut down towards the end of 1954. Breuer's successor as head of the German Association Shanghai, Hans W. Siegel, declared the Association annulled in April 1955.[47]

Early in 1952, Breuer had applied for his exit permit. His farewell party at the German Residents' Association was held on the 18th of April, but shortly afterwards his permit was revoked. During the following three months, he was questioned by the Increase-Production & Austerity Committee of the Peoples' Municipal Government. This was part of the "Five-Anti" Campaign—against bribery, tax evasion, theft of government property, fraud in government contracts and misuse of government business information for personal gain. Breuer called it "*Beichtzeit*" (confession time) and observed that suicides by Chinese and foreigners had become common in those days: 'by forcing each individual to testify something, entire chains of complaints are created, drawing more and more people into the maelstrom'.[48]

He was interrogated approximately 25 times 'very severely', so he wrote, but was always allowed to go home afterwards and was never physically maltreated. The questions asked concerned Melchers' property. As the last Melchers representative, he was held responsible for their real estate holdings, some of them still under Chinese cover, and for financial dealings. He was also questioned in connection with his work for the Residents' Association. His interrogators would not believe that it was voluntary work; it was presumed that he was a paid agent of the German government. He was finally cleared in early August 1952 and his exit permit was reissued on the 9th of August, on condition that he leave China within eight days. He found the time to visit the grave of one of his best friends, Melchers' partner Dr Adalbert Korff, who had died of leukaemia at the age of forty-five in March 1945. Most of his luggage had already been sent abroad. Valuables, letters and photographs of old China had to stay behind. Breuer was now in transition from "Old China Hand" to refugee; one of those who, having lost their adopted home, were heading for an unfamiliar homeland.

A POST-CHINA LIFE

He went to Germany via Hong Kong, where he stayed for six weeks, meeting "big shots" like Michael Jebsen of Jebsen & Co., Melchers' representative Rudolf Voremberg, members of the Kwok family (Wing On) and Sir John Keswick of Jardine, Matheson & Co.[49] Travelling via Bangkok, the city of his birth, Rome and Zurich, Breuer arrived in Hanover where his brother had prepared a flat for him, but left almost immediately for Hamburg, to give a lecture on the situation and morale in China. That was on the 27th of October 1952, on invitation of the OAV Hamburg, and in the presence of officials from the Foreign Office. Breuer stressed the Chinese government's success in dealing with corruption and the heightened standard of living of peasants and other formerly very poor parts of the population. He emphasised that the new government had the support of the people (with the exception of the big landowners) and outlined that he thought it highly unlikely that this government would just disappear—as former Chinese governments had. In all, he painted a cautiously optimistic picture of the new China.[50]

In February 1953, during an Agape celebration hosted by the Ostasiatischer Verein in Hamburg, he received a distinguished decoration for his endeavours as Chairman of the German community and his successful efforts in bringing destitute Germans out of China: the Commander's Cross of the Order of Merit of the Federal Republic of Germany. Professor Hallstein presented the medal on behalf of Federal President Theodor Heuss. In his address he said:

> Mr Breuer was in an extremely difficult situation which he mastered with great tact and ability for the benefit of his countrymen and German prestige. As the head of the German Association he was held responsible by the

Chinese administration for the actions of all German nationals, his position being that of a Consul without exequatur. With no regard towards his own personal safety, he successfully advocated the cause of Germans in China.[51]

(Translation by author)

When Hermann Breuer arrived in Germany in October 1952, he was almost 69 years of age and had lost a considerable amount of his savings. Also, his son was gravely ill following an accident as a paratrooper during the war (he died in 1956). As a grandfather, Breuer felt responsible for his three grandchildren. But this was not the only reason he was glad to be offered the paid post of consultant to the administrative body dealing with compensation for property lost in South East Asia. It was his job to assess claims or find people who could do so. This post allowed him to keep in touch with his former network and gave him the opportunity to help people with legitimate claims. Also, his personal experience meant that he could amiably explain refusals, and sometimes find other ways to help. It was a full time job that he held for ten years, subsequently working as a consultant on an advisory committee with the Federal Ministry for Exiles *(Bundesministerium für Angelegenheiten der Vertriebenen)*.

In 1954 Breuer was elected chairman of the OAV Bremen. In this capacity, he was able to assist in rebuilding Germany's trade connections with the Far East and could even contribute to the renewal of economic contacts with the People's Republic of China. When an official Chinese Trade Delegation headed by Dr Ji Chaoding, vice-president of the Committee for the Promotion of International Trade, visited Bremen, Breuer took part in the tour of the port areas under reconstruction, as well as the festive program for the guests and the discussions.[52] The German return visit in September 1957 to Beijing brought the signing of a first trade treaty between the People's Republic and Germany, fifteen years ahead of the re-establishment of diplomatic relations in 1972.

Breuer's humanity and his humour made him loved and honoured, until his death a few weeks before his ninetieth birthday, on the 24th of November 1973.

Christine Maiwald (christine.maiwald@t-online.de) studied German

Philology and History of Art in Hamburg and Vienna. She served in the cultural administrations of Hamburg, and was seconded to London before running marketing departments at the Hamburg Museums of Ethnology and of Applied Arts. Since her retirement, she has extensively researched the German experience in China in archives in Germany, London and Shanghai. She has published articles on the German Amateur Dramatic Society Shanghai and on the resurrection of the German community after the First World War. A comprehensive study of the life and work of German merchants in China during the first half of the 20th century, Das schwierige schöne Leben: Ein deutscher Kaufmann in Shanghai. 1906-1952, *has her great-uncle Hermann W. Breuer at its centre.*

———◇◇◇———

REFERENCES

1 Mechthild Leutner: Deutscher Dolmetscher in Kiautschou, jüdischer Exilant in Kunming: Erich Michelsens Leben als Kapitel deutsch-chinesischer Beziehungen', *China in a Global Context: Perspectives on and from China,* 50 (2018), 51–83 (p.51).

2 Breuer Family Archive, Breuer in a letter to his daughter-in-law, 2 July 1947.

3 Melchers Archive, Hong-Lists and photographs, C. Melchers & Co. KG, Bremen (private archive).

4 Breuer Family Archive, Breuer to his daughter-in-law, January 1964.

5 Wartime form for requesting money from one's own account held by the Shanghai Library, Bibliotheca Zi-Ka-Wei / Xujiahu 015794.

6 Christine Maiwald, 'Resurrection of the German community in Shanghai after the First World War and how Chinese Friends laid the Foundation Stones', Journal of the Royal Asiatic Society China, 77 (2017), pp. 143-161.

7 Breuer Family Archive, Photographs Breuer and staff at the Melchers building on Jiujiang Lu, 1924.

8 Breuer Family Archive, Breuer to his daughter-in-law when she faced divorce, remembering his own experience, 30 May 1947 (Translation by author).

9 *North China Herald,* 12 April 1932.

10 Paper Importers Association 'A Successful First Year: Cooperation with Chinese Guild: The Luxury Guild' *North China Herald,* 27 February 1926, Meetings Section, pp. 360-391.

11 Politisches Archiv des Auswärtigen Amtes (PA AA), Berlin, II Bd 2453 p. 253-256.

12 Christine Maiwald, 'Man spielt Theater hier im Fernen Osten. Der Deutsche Theater-Verein Shanghai.' *StuDeO-Info* June 2017, pp. 3-8 and *Studeo-Info* December 2017, pp. 29-35.

13 Today's commemorative plague is on Yuanmingyuan Lu where the stage door once was. In 1931 a new building for the Lyceum Theatre was opened at the corner of Changle Lu, Maoming Nan Lu. This building still stands today, it is a listed monument.

14 Entry for Melchers & Co. in the Hong-Lists from 1929.

15 Breuer Family Archive, letter home 10 September 1931 and Breuer: History of Melchers Shanghai (1941), Bundesarchiv, Akten der Heimatauskunftstelle, 7-34 / 116, p. 6.

16 Breuer Family Archive, Radio station: letter home 12 December 1930 and Geheimes Staatsarchiv Preußischer Kulturbesitz, HA Rep. 120 MfHuG, Abt. C XIII 18 Nr. 1 Bd. 28.

17 Hermann Breuer, *Firmengeschichte*, 1941, in BundesArchiv, Bundesarchiv, 7-34/116.

18 Carl Gerhard Melchers, *Antrag auf Lastenausgleich*, 15 March 1954, Anlage zu Beiblatt 4, in Bundesarchiv, 7-34 / 116.

19 *China Press*, 28 May 1929; also see detailed description of the building in Bundesarchiv, 7-34/116.

20 *The Shanghai Times*, 24 July 1931.

21 *Frankfurter Zeitung*, 4 May 1935.

22 *Liangyou* (*The Young Companion*) 114 (15 February 1936), Advertisement, p. 41.

23 Breuer Family Archive, Breuer in a letter to his brother, 25 August 1936.

24 Melchers Archive (private archive).

25 Kurtz und Knapp, 'Vor 85 Jahren: Nürnberger Gesetze erlassen', Reichsgesetzblatt, 1935, Nr. 125, S. 1134ff und Schautafel: https://www.bpb.de/kurz-knapp/hintergrund-aktuell/501380/vor-85-jahren-nuernberger-gesetze-erlassen/, [accessed 07 November 2023].

26 Peter Holzberger, *Recollections of an "Old China Hand"*. Hong Kong: Martin & Thomas, 1984, p. 75.

27 Melchers Archive, letter from Wing On Textile Company to the Enemy Property Affairs Commission, Shanghai (no date, c. second half of 1946). Bundesarchiv 7-34/116.

28 Breuer Family Archive, Breuer to his brother Karl, 19 August 1939.

29 Christine Maiwald, *Das schwierige schöne Leben: Ein deutscher Kaufmann in Shanghai. 1906-1952.* Hamburg, Munich: Dölling und Galitz, 2021, p. 339. Advertisement in North China Daily News 31 December 1939, p. 1.

30 North China Daily News, 18 July 1947, Letter to the Editor signed 'Disgusted Briton'. The post was sent when Breuer's deportation as a Nazi was imminent.

31 National Archives and Records Administration (NARA), RG 226, E 182, Box 23, F 122.

32 Breuer Family Archive, Breuer, Memorandum (private note), 22 July 1968.

33 Klaus Mehnert, *Ein Deutscher in der Welt. Erinnerungen 1906-1981*, (Stuttgart: Europäische Bildungsgemeinschaft - Gütersloh: Bertelsmann-Club, 1984) pp. 306-307 and p. 405.

34 *China Press*, 1 July 1946, 'The United States notified the Chinese Government that it regarded as an un-friendly act the removal of 400 Germans from the American list of 'dangerous and objectionable Nazis'.

35 Christine Maiwald, *Leben*, p. 391 and p. 410.

36 NARA, RG 226, E 182, Box 23, F 122.

37 See lists of passenger: Bayerische Staatsbibliothek, BSB Ana 708: StuDeO 237 (Marine Robin, 7 July 1946, Shanghai passengers); StuDeO 330 (Marine Jumper, 7 and 11 February 1947); StuDeO 336 (General Black, 31 August 1947).

38 Breuer Family Archive, Breuer to his daughter-in-law, 18 October 1947.

39 Christine Maiwald, *Leben*, p. 556.

40 Christine Maiwald, *Leben*, p. 454.

41 Bernd Eberstein, *Der Ostasiatische Verein 1900-2000*, (Hamburg: Christians, 2000) p. 143.

42 Hermann W. Breuer, *Konsul ohne Exequatur*, in: Diplomatischer Kurier 2/1953, Heft 6, pp. 96-97.

43 PA AA MfA A A 6471, p. 2.

44 Christine Maiwald, *Leben*, p. 471, p.480, p. 487 and p. 529.

45 Lists in PA AA 514-01/13, 1949-1950, B 10, Band 1942, Fiche 5630.

46 Christine Maiwald, *Leben*, p. 486 and p. 492.

47 Hans Wilhelm Siegel, letter 10 May 1955 to OAV. Staatsarchiv Hamburg, Bestand 613-4/5, vol. 32.

48 Deutsche Gemeinde Shanghai an Ostasiatischen Verein Hamburg-Bremen, (March 1952); PA AA B10, 1944, A5637 G9.

49 Breuer Family Archive, Breuer, 4 September 1952 to Rolf Heyn.

50 Minutes, Ostasiatischer (Verein) Meeting, 31 October 1952, PA AA B85 235, s.p.

51 Bundesarchiv B122/38528 and PA AA B85 235, s.p.

52 Christine Maiwald, *Leben*, p. 49.

THE CELEBRITY RACEHORSE TRAINER
OF OLD SHANGHAI AND HONG KONG
By Paul Sofronoff

ABSTRACT

George Sofronoff left Russia and came to China in the 1930's; he was young, inexperienced, and full of optimism. After leaving his family behind, he got a job travelling with the ponies to Tsing Tao, eventually arriving in Shanghai in 1935. There, he became a racehorse trainer for some of the most well-known members of Shanghai's foreign community: David 'Nunkie' Sassoon, the black sheep of that famous family, and Eric Moller, the shipping magnate and owner of the largest stable of racehorses in Shanghai. George experienced early success, training winners of the Champions' Day Cup and Shanghai Derby, before travelling to Hong Kong and winning their Derby. George's first-hand accounts tell of these interesting times and the impact of World War II, providing a unique personal perspective, complimenting the well-known general history. It contains never published personal photos and personal documents.

FROM RUSSIA TO CHINA

My grandfather George Alexander Sofronoff (Georgiy Alexandrovich) was born in the small village of Duroy in County Zaibakal, Siberia, in Russia on 6 May 1910. He started looking after horses on the family farm from the age of 5. George recalled,

> It wasn't a bad life, really. My family lived right on the border. We traded with the Chinese. Selling a horse for some food or money. The horses were ponies, about 14 hands, and we would have Sunday races against our neighbours, keeping the best of the work horses for the racing.

The 'races' were on the dirt roads between villages.

In 1931, at age 21, George and his cousin Ivan Alexseevich and a few friends rode over the Argun river to the Chinese province of Heilongjiang. 'God bless you', said his father as he waved his son goodbye. Although he wrote to his brothers, he never returned to Russia. 'Go back to Siberia?' he later recalled, 'No, how can I go back? When I left I was young, only 21, and I knew nothing. I thought I would ride off for an adventure and then return, but once I was over the border, I knew I could never go back'.[1]

George ended up in the city of Hailar. The lifestyle was pretty much the same as it had been on the Siberian side of the Argun River, and there was no problem finding a job for a hard-working young farm boy, skilled in handling horses. In Hailar, horse racing, whilst important, was not organised. However, George recalled a $2000 wager on a race at this time, and that he took $100 in commission!

The next year the Japanese invaded China, but this caused little more than a ripple in the far north and life for George went on without interruption, 'We heard rumours of war, and we got a Russian language newspaper once a week from Harbin, but we were not really affected'. Russian horse traders would frequently visit the stables where he worked, to buy horses for the tracks and schools in Tientsin, Hankou, Hong Kong and Shanghai. One of them offered George a job, and in 1933 he saddled up again and rode off to Tsing Tao. George recalled,

> Tsing Tao was a beautiful city. There was exciting racing on Saturdays and Sundays with Mongolian ponies crossbred with Russian Horses. I was called 'Number One' which meant foreman, and I generally had to look after the horses and prepare them for the journeys by sea to their ultimate destinations.

The horses they raced in China at the time were not the thoroughbreds seen in Europe, America and Australia. Although they were called 'China Ponies', the horses came from Mongolia and stood less than 5 feet tall. Interestingly, it is hard to breed horses in much of China due to low levels of calcium in organic matter, including water. As George explained,

> China doesn't have the grass, doesn't have the soil. Mongolia was the breeding place for horses [...] They ran around half wild in herds of a thousand or more. Each stallion in the herd would take 40 or 50 of the mares into his own pack. He was the king of the pack because he was the biggest and the

strongest and the best fighter. [...] The foals, they grew up on the best grass you could get anywhere—just like Kentucky bluegrass. Maybe they were only ponies, but they had fire in their hearts, and they could carry big weights for long distances. They were real horses.[2]

SUCCESS IN SHANGHAI

In 1935, George was encouraged to head to Shanghai, where the horse racing was bigger, and the opportunities even more exciting. At this time, Shanghai was home to foreign concessions that came into existence in the wake of the First Opium War. The foreigners cut out sections of the city and made them their own. They brought their foreign laws, their own police and in time western architecture and facilities. Foreigners in Shanghai were not subject to Chinese law, but to the laws of their own countries. It was a de facto colony, but operating within the sovereign country of China. A strange quirk of history, given its own name, extra-territoriality.[3]

Figure 1: George in Tsing Tao, 1934

Shanghai was already home to many thousands of Russians when George arrived there. The Russian community in Shanghai grew from about 300 in 1906 to more than 25,000 by 1937. There were two Russian schools as well as a variety of cultural and sporting clubs. There were two Russian language newspapers, *Zaria* (Dawn) and *Slovo* (The Word), and a radio station. Russian tenancy and commerce was concentrated in Frenchtown. Avenue Joffre, now Huaihai Lu, became known as 'Little Russia' or 'Moscow Boulevard' for its cluster of Russian restaurants and shops.[4] By 1934, Russians formed the largest foreign community in Shanghai after the Japanese.

Eight out of ten foreign passers-by are Russians, speaking their mother tongue, entering Russian shops or restaurants with Russian sign boards and behaving generally as if they

Figure 2: Shanghai Emigrant Registration Card for Russians[8]

were exclusively amongst themselves.[5]

In 1921, the Soviet government denationalised all Russians who had left the motherland; they became stateless with no passport to allow them to travel anywhere else. As the rules of extra-territoriality were based on treaties they did not apply to stateless Russian émigrés. If arrested, they would be dealt with under Chinese law.[6] The Chinese Government required every Russian entering Shanghai to register within ten days with the local Bureau of Public Safety.[7]

The foreign community started racing in Shanghai in around 1845, these were mostly social events where owners rode their own horses. Official races started in 1847 and the Shanghai Racing Club was formed in 1850.[9] Lawrence Kadoorie recalled, 'Shanghai was a place where one could dance all night, go riding at 6 o'clock in the morning, work all day and yet, not feel tired'.[10]

George quickly found work as a stable boy to David E. 'Nunkie' Sassoon, uncle of business taipan Sir Victor Sassoon. David was the black sheep of the family and had a scandalous reputation as a philanderer and hard-nosed racing man. 'He spent most mornings studying racing papers and form books until eleven, when his valet served an admirably chilled, half bottle of bubbly'.[11] Nunkie had been originally given the job of managing Victor's 'Eve' racing stable, but a disagreement between the two on how to properly prepare the horses led to Nunkie forming his own opposition stable, cheekily called 'Morn', the opposite of 'Eve'.

In 1937, George married Valentina Bourtzeff, whose family had moved from Harbin after the Japanese occupied the city. Life was good for the young couple, but their happiness was soon to be overshadowed by Japan's ongoing war with China. In 1937, Japanese troops reached the outskirts of Shanghai. Crowds in the International Settlement gathered on rooftops to observe the fighting around them.

Approximately 2,000, mostly Chinese, civilians were killed; the date of 14 August 1937 becoming known as Bloody Saturday.[12] The battle lasted three months and some estimates put Chinese casualties as high as 300,000. The Japanese were careful to avoid the International Settlement and French Concession for fear of encouraging America and Britain to support China. Extraordinarily, racing resumed in December 1937.

Despite the war going on around them, the foreign concessions remained neutral, and separate. The term *gudao* 孤岛 or 'lone island' was coined to reference this extraordinary situation. The International Settlement actually went so far as to declare its neutrality from the war. More than a million Chinese refugees crowded into the nine square miles of the concessions, and horses from other race clubs were evacuated to the Shanghai Race Club facilities.

The neutral status of the foreign concessions was dependent on Japan choosing not to do anything that would offend the British or Americans. Japanese sentries stood at the Hongkou side of the Garden Bridge and required everyone coming or going into the International Settlement to bow to them, and if their bows were deemed insufficiently differential, they were punished. Even the trams that ran down the middle of the bridge were required to stop, and the occupants compelled to bow.[13] The driver had to request permission to cross in Japanese, sometimes 'he would twist his syllables so that the sentence came out as a Shanghainese obscenity enjoining the Japanese

Figure 3: Nunkie Sassoon leads in *Radiant Morn*

sentry to do something dire to his mother'.[14]

In May 1938, George celebrated twin successes. His son Alexander, my father, was born and Nunkie Sassoon won his fifth Champions' Day Stakes, with his horse *Radiant Morn*. Just ten days later, Nunkie passed away and his stable was liquidated. He left instructions to be buried in an 'elegant casket of crystal and gold'.[15] George had a new family to support and no job.

He was quick to find alternative employment as the Stable Master at the Columbia and Great Western Riding Academy, managing 225 horses groomed for social riding. The Riding Academy was associated with the Columbia Country Club which had been established by the American community. It was located about 20 minutes drive from the business district of Shanghai and was described in a guidebook as 'really in the country'. Later in the war, the Club was used by the Japanese as an internment camp.

Later in 1938, George was offered the job of deputy trainer at the 'Mr Cire's' stable, owned by shipping taipan, Eric Moller, the largest stable in Shanghai. Moller was the chair of the Racing Club, and had been involved in racing for many years, including riding many winners in Shanghai and Hong Kong; he even rode for the legendary Sir Catchick Paul Chater in Hong Kong. Only a month after George arrived, the head trainer was sacked. Moller challenged the recently arrived George. 'Are you married, boy?'. George remembered: 'I couldn't speak much English, but I understood what he wanted. He told me if I worked hard, he would help me and offered me a job as senior trainer'.

So, at age 28, George was in charge of a large and influential stable. George soon had success with his team. In November 1938, *Merrylight* won a prime race on the calendar, the Autumn Champions' Day Stakes. This was Moller's first Champions' win. He had been racing horses in Shanghai for decades, but he had never won the Champions'.[16] While plaudits went to the jockey, Eric's son, Ralph 'Boogie' Moller, there is a short reference in the *China Press*, to a man 'behind the scenes, pulling strings'. It should be noted that, in this era of gentlemen amateurs, the trainer was not mentioned in race results,

> In studying the jockey records one would attribute the success of the Moller stable to the fine riding of the three Moller brothers, but one should look behind the scenes

Figure 4: *Merrylight* led by Mrs and Mr Moller, George is far left

for there are two important persons who are equally responsible for this sensational winning streak. These men are Eric Moller, and the Russian head groom and trainer (we don't know his name). Credit must go to them in maintaining their ponies in top-fitness, for a long season interspersed with gruelling contests.[17]

In 1939, the Sofronoff trained *Joylight* caused a big upset by winning the Shanghai Derby.[18] George trained two more Shanghai Derby winners before racing ended there in 1942.

A YEAR IN HONG KONG

In 1939-40, George first travelled to Hong Kong, taking 6 horses from the Moller stable. They collected several trophies, and in February 1940, *Satinlight* won the Hong Kong Derby in record time.[19]

Valentina and Alexander had remained in Shanghai where, in 1940, the British and Americans decided that the International Settlement was indefensible and withdrew their small military forces. Over 8,000 British citizens continued to live and work in Shanghai, alongside nearly 2,000 Americans, more than 25,000 White Russian émigrés, 18,000 Jews who had escaped Nazi persecution, and millions of Chinese seeking safety from the war.[20] It seems hard to understand in hindsight, but the 'bubble' of neutrality surrounding the International Settlement remained in place all the way up to the spring race meeting of 1941.

In September 1941, George made the decision to strike out on his own and take a role as a trainer in Hong Kong. It was a decision that Eric Moller characterised as 'unsatisfactory treatment to the Owner who has taught his trainer so much' in a personal reference he supplied. George arrived in Hong Kong expecting that his wife and son would shortly follow. But once again, the Japanese Army interfered with the Sofronoff family's plans.

On 8 December 1941, shortly after their planes attacked Pearl Harbour, the Japanese invaded the foreign concessions in Shanghai, facing little to no resistance. Even then, horse racing continued, although now under the direction of the occupying, Japanese forces.

> As it had been for a century, Shanghai remained atypical: in the midst of humanity's deadliest war, Shanghai was relatively quiet. Quiet enough to watch horse races. [21]

Hong Kong was also occupied by the Japanese, and, frantically, George tried to make his way back to his family in Shanghai. It was not until March 1942 that he was able to book passage on a ship heading north. He had become friendly with a fellow Russian trainer, Tokmakoff. With the Hong Kong banks shut, George gave his remaining Hong Kong dollars to him. Whilst he appreciated it, Tokmakoff wondered how he would ever find a way to repay George. 'The bloody Japanese robbed me properly', George recalled wryly.

> I lined up to get a ticket and the Japanese ticket agent asked me if I had money. I said yes and he asked what sort. I told him I had Hong Kong dollars and he said they were no good and I had to change it to Japanese gold yen [...] I did this at an enforced terrible rate of exchange and lost half my money. Then I went back to get the ticket and the Japanese official smiled and said I had to have *military* yen. [...] So I had to cash in gold yen for military yen and once again I got robbed of more than half of my money, but at least I got a passage on a ship. [22]

It turned out to be a lucky ship. It got to Shanghai. The next two ships that attempted the trip were sunk by submarines, with great loss of life. George was reunited with his wife and young son.

The family moved from Bubbling Well Road to Great Western Road and gated rows of one and a half storey townhouses. My father, at the time still a young boy, later recalled:

> The ground floor had a large dining room and a primitive laundry/bathroom with a huge pot (glazed on the outside; it was originally used for fermenting various foods). I used to enjoy my bath in that pot every evening. On the mezzanine floor we had a small room which was used for overnight stays by friends and relatives. On the first floor, we had two bedrooms—one for me and one for my parents. [...] My father, when he came home in the evening, would read the news in the Russian paper and hear the news on the radio, also in Russian. One oddity I remember was my father saw a rat and decided to shoot it with an air rifle! I can't remember whether he got it or missed.

In October 1942, the Japanese announced that the racecourse and Club were to be closed indefinitely. 'Enemy nationals', including Eric Moller were arrested and placed in internment camps for the remainder of the war.[23] Russia and Japan did not formally become enemies until near the end of the war, and so the Sofronoffs remained outside the camps, but still subject to harsh restrictions, and hyperinflation. George had a close brush with a Japanese officer brandishing a pistol. He did as he was told, bowing low and apologising, and was allowed to walk on.

George went back to giving lessons in his own business, the Lincoln Riding School. Even though times were tough the family was always able to afford food and the occasional treat.

My father remembered playing with Chinese children in the local neighbourhood and becoming fluent in Shanghainese. His fondest memories were of the various street foods he ate, including chòu dòufu 臭豆腐, da bing 大饼 pancakes and youtiao 油条, strings of dough fried in boiling oil and then twirled by vendor into an elongated shape. These oily and very hot food items were wrapped in newspaper and usually eaten straight away. When he returned to Shanghai in 2010, he excitedly led me and my brothers on street food expeditions.

On 16 August 1945, the race track was again the centre of attention as Japanese officers assembled to listen to the Emperor's announcement of surrender. A few weeks later, American and Chinese forces arrived in Shanghai to take control. Unexpectedly, they also announced the end of extra-territoriality and foreign concessions in China. For the first time in more than a hundred years, China controlled the entire city of Shanghai.

Racing in Shanghai was at an end, and in time the Race Club donated its land and buildings to pay off debts and taxes. The Clubhouse building still remains to this day and is fittingly, the Shanghai History Museum. The space around it is now the People's Square and Park.

DISPLACED PEOPLE

In 1949, the Sofronoff family like many other stateless Russians, found themselves in a tent on the small island of Tubabao in the Philippines. George recalled, 'All we knew was that we were heading for a displaced persons camp in the Philippines. Just where it was and what was going to happen to us after that, we had no idea'.[24] In a cruel twist of fate, the Hong Kong Jockey Club (HKJC) offered George a job at the same time, but, as a refugee, he did not meet the requirements of the Immigration Department.

Figure 5: In front of tent 12 on Tubabao Island. George is second from the right.

In September 1949, the Sofronoffs were offered a place in Brisbane, Australia. All applicants had to sign a commitment to work in jobs directed by the Australian Government for two years. They would secure citizenship after 5 years residence, a step that was key to George finding a way to get back to Hong Kong to train horses. Speaking very little English and apparently unskilled, George was only offered menial jobs.

> For two years, we new arrivals had to work under contract. My first job was cutting down trees for firewood. After four months of that, the Government moved us to Enoggera and each day we would be loaded on a bus. I was working as a labourer in an army camp. There was nothing much to do. They gave us some sticks with feathers on the end and told us to get the dust off a dockside warehouse. But all we did was fish for mullet and when an officer appeared, the foreman would call out "Captain coming" and we would all leap up to get the dust flying. Then the officer would go away and we would put down our dusters and pick up our fishing lines again.[25]

George and Valentina were also blessed with a daughter and second son during these years in Brisbane.

As soon as he was naturalised, George wrote to his friends in Hong Kong saying, 'I'm a free man!' In 1956, the Hong Kong Jockey Club offered George a probationary trainer's licence. The only thing holding him back was the airfare. Fortunately, Mr Tokmakoff had a chance to repay George's earlier kindness, and wired him the money. The wartime debt was repaid!

RETURN TO HONG KONG

George jumped on a plane and his horse training career resumed in January 1956. He began with 12 horses, but by the end of year had doubled his team. It didn't take him long to have success. At the halfway mark of the season, the *South China Morning Post* correspondent 'Blinkers', noted that,

> Another who is expected to do better as the season progresses is newcomer George Sofronoff. After an

indifferent start, when he seemed to be doing everything else but saddling winners, Sofronoff is at last finding his stride.

By the end of the season, he had saddled 14 winners—a record for a trainer in their freshman year.[26]

In the next season, 1957-58, he was the leading trainer in Hong Kong. A title he was to hold for nine consecutive seasons. So dominant was he, that in 1968, the HKJC introduced a new rule restricting the number of horses in a stable to 45. Overnight, George's stable strength halved. Later he was allotted only one Griffin because owners were flocking to him with their horses. Griffins were new horses, yet to race, a nickname borrowed from India, where the term referred to a new European arrival to the country. His success had led the Race Club management to fear that no other trainer would get a chance.

The newspapers called him 'Genial George' or the 'Siberian Supremo'. He was a dominant figure in Hong Kong racing for many years. When asked to explain his success, George talked about preparation: 'I believe in giving my charges plenty of work'. He also spoke about diet in a way that was different to other trainers of the time, who fed all horses the same thing every day. 'Every horse needs to be fed differently. Some may eat 15lbs, others 7lbs. A study of their work and their feeding provides a good guide to their fitness'.

In 1971, the HKJC turned professional, inviting overseas trainers and jockeys to come to Hong Kong. Competition became much keener, and no single stable could dominate as it had in the past. The good horses no longer automatically came to George, indeed the Jockey Club virtually directed owners to stable their horses with newly appointed trainers from abroad.[27] But even with this increased competition, he continued to perform well, finishing in the top three, seven times in nine years.

When international jockeys came to Hong Kong, the best of the best rode George's horses, including Lester Piggott, Pat Eddery, Willie Carson and Yves St. Martin. When Willie Carson later became a trainer, he asked George if he could name one of his horses *Sofronoff*. George also supported many local riders and gave maestro Tony Cruz his first win on *Cirrus*.

Although still a successful trainer, George was forced to retire at the HKJC's mandatory retirement age of 70. Despite lobbying by loyal

Figure 6: The 1979 Hong Kong Derby

owners and racing fans, no extension was forthcoming. Of course, George went out on top, winning a third Hong Kong Derby in his final season, and saddling up a winner on his last race day, 30 May 1980.

In 1982, George was asked how many winners he had saddled up as a trainer in Hong Kong. He admitted that he did not know, 'Quite a few. Quite a few'. Official sources did keep score, and the HKJC confirmed that the total is 724.

A MAN OF CHARACTER

George passed away on 27 July 1987 aged 77, surrounded by family and friends. For most of his life he lived and worked in countries that were foreign to him and that regarded him as an outsider. Countries in which he had to battle with the language. Yet he succeeded, for despite his inability to speak the local language, whether it was Chinese or English, there was something about George that attracted people to him. His character and integrity led to many lifelong friendships and enabled him to endure and rise above hardship, separation and destitution.

Paul Sofronoff has a Bachelor of Laws, a Masters of Law and Masters of Business Administration. He has published a number of articles and book chapters on topics related to the law. Paul is the grandson of the subject of this article, George. He spent several enjoyable early mornings with his grandfather at the Happy Valley Racecourse as a young boy. In 2010 Paul travelled to Shanghai with his father as a guide.

—∞∞—

REFERENCES

1. Kevin Sinclair, Siberian trainer's long ride to adventure, 30 May 1982 *South China Morning Post* p.10.
2. Geoff Somers, (ed.). *The Royal Hong Kong Jockey Club* (Michael Stevenson, 1975), p. 24.
3. Robert Bickers, Shanghailanders: The Formation and Identity of the British Settler Community in Shanghai, 1843-1937, *Past and Present* 159 (May 1988): 161-211, pp.165-166.
4. Paul French, *The Old Shanghai A-Z*, (HKU Press, 2010).
5. Ellen Thorbecke, Shanghai (with sketches by Frederic Schiff), *North China Daily News & Herald* (1940).
6. A. Kamalakaran, Russian Noon: A look at white émigré life in 1930's Shanghai, Russia Beyond, 18 Sep 2015 <https://www.rbth.com/arts/2015/09/18/russian_noon_a_look_at_white_emigre_life_in_1930s_shanghai_49337.html> see also Katya Knyazeva, High and Low: The Material Culture of the Russian Diaspora in Shanghai, 1920s-1950s, Global Histories Vol III (Oct 2017), pp. 21-41.
7. E.H. Anstice, Shanghai's White Russians, *Contemporary Review* (Feb 1937) pp. 215-220.
8. Microfilm copy of Russian emigrant registration cards and certificates 1940–1952, National Archives and Records Administration USA, Group 263.2.3. (courtesy Katya Knyazeva).
9. Austin Coates, *China Races* (Oxford Uni Press, 1983), p. 27.
10. Jonathon Kaufman, *The Last Kings of Shanghai: The Rival Jewish Dynasties that Helped Create Modern China*, (Viking 2020), p. 97.
11. Joseph Sassoon, *The Global Merchants: The Enterprise and Extravagance of the Sassoon Dynasty,* (Allen Lane, 2022), p. 212.
12. Paul French, *Bloody Saturday: Shanghai's Darkest Day*, (Penguin Specials, 2017), see also Peter Harmsen, *Shanghai 1937: Stalingrad on the Yangtze*, (Casemate, 2013).
13. Stella Dong, *Shanghai. The Rise and Fall of a Decadent City* (W.Morrow, 2001), p. 257.
14. Lynn Pan. *In Search of Old Shanghai* (Joint Publishing, Hong Kong, 1983), p. 36.
15. Sassoon *Global Merchants* p. 253.

16. James Carter, *Champions Day: The End of Old Shanghai* (W.W. Norton, 2020), p. 174 and see also The Chaser, Merrylight wins Champions: Magnificent Finish Leaves Gold Vase Second, *The North China Herald*, 16 Nov 1938, p. 285.

17. David Zenter, Sports Reflections: Biggest Champions' Crowd for Seven Years, *The China Press*, 11 Nov 1938, p. 6.

18. The Chaser, Shanghai Spring Race Meeting, *North China Herald*, 10 May 1939, p.250.

19. https://www.racingmemorieshk.com/hottopics/moller-racing/ This website is no longer live, but can be accessed via the *Wayback Machine* at <Web Archive>, see also Mr Moller Celebrates Derby Victory, The North China Herald, 28 Feb 1940, p.341.

20. M. Felton, Japanese Take Shanghai's International Settlement <https://www.thatsmags.com/shanghai/post/21706/this-day-in-history-japanese-take-international-settlement>.

21. Carter *Champions Day*, p.260.

22. Sinclair, Siberian trainer's long ride.

23. M. Felton, Japanese Take Shanghai's International Settlement.

24. Sinclair, Siberian trainer's long ride.

25. Bart Sinclair, Meet Turf's Manchurian Candidate *The Daily Sun*, 7 August 1982 p.90.

26. *Blinkers,* Racing Comments, *South China Morning Post,* 26 Mar 1957.

27. P. Metrevelli, RHKJC ban on big stables may be lifted, *South China Morning Post*, 16 June 1971, p.15.

SECTION 4

Reviews and Passages

THE PEKING EXPRESS: THE BANDITS WHO STOLE A TRAIN, STUNNED THE WEST, AND BROKE THE REPUBLIC OF CHINA

By James M. Zimmerman

Public Affairs, 2023

Reviewed by Frances Wood

On 5 May 1923, bandits attacked and derailed the Shanghai-Peking express train, forcing a group of (mainly) foreign hostages up a mountain in Shandong province and holding them captive for 37 days. This story made headlines all over the world; although hostage-taking was rife in China at the time, with 92 incidents reported in Shandong province alone by the end of 1923.

The passengers on the Shanghai-Peking express that night, enjoying the luxury of the new overnight train with its comfortable sleeping berths and drawing room car, included the admirable journalist and editor of the *China Weekly Review*, John B. Powell; Guiseppe Musso, an Italian lawyer, representative of the Shanghai Opium Merchant's Combine and later to become a propagandist film-maker for Mussolini; two American servicemen based in Tianjin, travelling with their wives and young sons; a Frenchman, a senior officer in the Chinese Salt Administration; a group of Shanghai businessmen with interests ranging from selling fast cars to exporting mah-jong sets; and a stout, well-dressed woman, Lucy Aldrich, sister-in-law of John D. Rockefeller, heir to the fortune of the Standard Oil Company which was widely involved in China. Miss Aldrich was on her second circumnavigation of the globe, accompanied by her secretary and a French maid. In the luxury of the train, all seemed impervious to any threat, even the long-term residents of Shanghai, who might have suspected that it was the interior of China that was dangerous, not the modern, east coast.

Stopped at a station in the middle of the night, Powell was surprised to see what looked like a lot of Japanese passengers leaving the train, provoking much speculation later as to Japanese involvement. But it was further down the line that a local bandit, Sun Meiyao, led his troops to loosen the rails, causing carriages to overturn. Thrown from their bunks, the passengers were attacked by bandit soldiers forcing them out, many barefoot and wearing pyjamas and night dresses, pushing them along stony tracks away from the train, whilst other bandits looted as much as they could.

Using a mass of surviving material from Powell's meticulous account, diaries, memoirs and memorabilia, Zimmerman recounts the trials of the succeeding weeks in vivid detail. The passenger hostages were divided into groups: Miss Aldrich was separated from her maid and spent time trying to call on help from Standard Oil; in filthy villages where she was well-treated by poverty-stricken women who had no idea what oil was, let alone Standard Oil. She managed to hide her jewels amongst some rocks and, amazingly, they were later retrieved with the help of one of the bandits who had been guarding her. Families were torn apart, the two small sons of the American military men showed considerable courage, all suffered from inadequate clothing, though many were provided with a strange assortment of garments looted from the train, and all found the hard, flavourless dry breads they were given almost impossible to eat. Shot at and harried by warlord troops from near the railway line, divided into separate groups, they were driven up towards the bandits' mountain stronghold.

Such was the publicity given to the event that a support mission was quickly set up by the indefatigable Carl Crow, Shanghai newspaperman, businessman and advertising pioneer. He eventually presided over a daily round of some 30 to 40 coolies carrying corned beef, potatoes, onions, tinned fruit, sugar, salt, bread, biscuits, cheese, jam, butter, toothbrushes, underwear, soap, toilet paper, cigars, writing materials, books, cameras, bottled water and camp beds.

At the same time, the embarrassed Chinese government asked an American advisor, Roy Scott Anderson, to negotiate the hostages' freedom. Negotiation was massively complex. The central government in Peking had no control over the local warlord Tien Chung-yu whose troops harassed and killed the bandits and their hostages, and little control over the Peking warlord Ts'ao K'un who was planning a military coup. Sun Meiyao, the bandit leader, could have been seen as just another warlord but he was different. A sort of Robin Hood, he could be seen as a 'hao han', an archetypical tough guy, but with a heart of some gold, of the sort encountered in Chinese traditional fiction, in novels such as Shuihu juan/The Water Margin. Sun was fighting against corrupt officialdom in his home area where his own brother, a quiet intellectual, had been murdered by Tien Chung-yu. Sun and many of his men were soldiers who had been discharged (unpaid) and abandoned and, when it came to negotiations with Roy Anderson, Sun asked that his men be taken back into the army, clothed, fed and paid and formed into a 'Self-Governed Army for the Establishment of the Country'.

Anderson achieved agreement to the mass pardon and though he was unable to get all the foreign powers involved—France, Britain, the USA, Holland, Denmark and Italy—to agree to guarantee the arrangements, Sun accepted Anderson's own guarantee instead. There was also a separate financial negotiation by Du Yuesheng and it took several more weeks for Chinese hostages to be released. Within months, however, on 19 December, Sun was murdered by Tien Chung-yu's replacement and all the soldiers in his new brigade were killed or dismissed. Anderson was already aware of the continuing and dangerous turmoil around China's leadership for as he returned to Peking in mid-June, he witnessed the exile of president Li who had been dismissed by none other than Ts'ao K'un, whose own presidency would not last a year.

Anderson, who felt that an agreement was an agreement, was distressed and sickened by Sun's murder. His despair is reminiscent of that of General Gordon during the Taiping rebellion. Having defeated the Taipings in Suzhou in 1863, Gordon had given his word that their leaders would be spared. The Chinese government immediately executed them all. Gordon was found in 'hysterical tears' holding up the severed head of one of the Taiping kings. His word had meant nothing to the Chinese government, and Anderson's personal guarantee was treated with similar contempt. And though Gordon survived, Anderson died in mysterious circumstances in Peking in 1925.

The Peking Express is great fun to read with its unlikely cast of characters stumbling in their night clothes up a Shandong mountain. It benefits from the rich variety of first-hand accounts and the variety of personalities. It has also benefited from James Zimmerman's enthusiasm in tracking down materials and informants and the sites themselves, clambering through nettles along railway lines and ascending to the mountain stronghold, by cable-car now. He conveys his sense of outrage at the betrayal of Anderson's painfully negotiated deal and it is a worrying betrayal. Whilst Sun Meiyao was hardly a hero, his actions on behalf of his poverty-stricken and desperate soldier-bandits do stand in marked contrast to the self-seeking ambition and duplicity of those in greater power such as Ts'ao K'un.

Frances Wood studied Chinese at the universities of Cambridge, Peking and London. She worked in the SOAS library before moving to the British Library as Curator of the Chinese collections. Her books include The Blue Guide to China, Did Marco Polo Go to China?, The Silk Road *and* No Dogs and Not Many Chinese: Treaty Port Life in China 1843-1943.

CHINESE DREAMS IN ROMANTIC ENGLAND: THE LIFE AND TIMES OF THOMAS MANNING

By Edward Weech

Manchester University Press, 2022

Reviewed by Paul French

The tricky question faced by Thomas Manning (1772-1840) in England in the early 1800s was how to study China when nobody much knew anything. He had no great libraries to consult, no Chinese Studies departments at Oxford or Cambridge to attend. Nothing more than a random and eclectic range of sources in Latin, Portuguese, French, Italian and Chinese, the latter of which he could not initially read. He did have Marco Polo, du Halde's collection of the writings of the Peking Jesuits, and some observations of those recently returned from the new Canton 'Factories'. Learning the language was a long, laborious, and virtually impossible task—no teachers, no flashcards, no one else to talk to in Chinese! Even Chinese objects were relatively rare in museums prior to the Opium Wars. The East India Company (EIC), that at that time largely controlled the early China trade, was suspicious and often downright unhelpful to those not directly linked to trade. Manning was aware that some foreigners had been expelled or imprisoned by the Chinese for attempting to learn the language—outlawed at that time.

'China' was an almost impossible task. Weech shows that to show a keen interest, as Manning did, was seen by many in England, and also among the foreigners enduring the Canton Factories in order to get wealthy, as 'simply odd, complex, quixotic'. Manning was, according to contemporaries who knew him in England and later in Canton, all those things—perhaps as Sinologists have long tended to be!

This fascinating and highly readable account of Thomas Manning's lifelong quest to know China is by Edward Weech, the Librarian at the RAS in London. The RAS Library in Euston holds the bulk of the sources Weech uses to reconstruct Manning's life, including his quite voluminous correspondence. We see how he began the daunting process of investigating China. Manning was a polymath and a member of the then forward-thinking, if not perhaps quite revolutionary then at least quite varied, English group of artists, writers, poets, and philosophers known collectively as the Romantics. Weech dubs Manning as developing a 'radical orientalism'. This approach to China was developed by a number of Romantics in England who evinced an interest in China, as well as some others stationed in Macao and Canton with the East India Company.

We often tend to over identify the Romantics solely with a bucolic notion of the English countryside—Wordsworth, Coleridge, Lamb. However, there was always an interest in the 'East' among this loose group.

The focus of their interest may have been the Near East, but in works such as, most notably, Coleridge's poem *Kubla Khan* (completed in 1797 and published in 1816) we see that their fascinations stretched further. Charles Lamb had begun a collection of Chinoiserie and Chinese ceramics. The Romantics took an interest in 'ordinary people', rural life and customs and, in the form of Thomas Manning, this extended to the peoples of China.

Without easy travel options and lacking a vast array of written or visual sources to pore over, how does one come to any sort of understanding of China? Manning's answer, and his major life struggle for many years, was to immerse himself as totally as possible in China, to 'Orientalise' himself—absorb China as best he could, everywhere he could, and acquire knowledge and understanding as if by osmosis. Manning sought out and encountered most of those interested in China in the early 1800s—the proto-Sinologues, religious evangelicals, the plain curious, and the adventurers who gravitated towards the China Trade to make their fortunes. All, missionaries to chancers, relied for their passage and access on the East India Company. The EIC was the only game in town if you were interested in the Far East and the EIC was interested in anyone with any knowledge of China, however vague or limited. The EIC, and by extension Britain, had growing commercial interests in China and needed market intel to secure its forward position.

Weech's page-turning opening to his biography of Manning jumps ahead to 1811 when we encounter our subject in Tibet, forty years after the Scottish adventurer and EIC diplomat George Bogle visited, but still phenomenally early. Manning, after failing to slip in via Canton, is attempting a roundabout route to China, heading into Tibet, donning bushy beard and Chinese robes as a disguise. To no end—as soon as

Manning reached Lhasa, he was expelled by the Chinese Amban who suspected him of being either a Christian missionary, an EIC spy, or both.

Where did Manning's interest in China, which soon morphed into an obsession, come from given that he was not commercially minded, a saver of souls or, particularly a profiteering adventurer? Weech suggests his initial point of contact was a theatre production Manning saw as a boy in the 1780s of Arthur Murphy's *Orphan of China,* an adaptation of Voltaire's adaptation of a Yuan Dynasty play, *The Orphan of Zhao,* attributed to the thirteenth-century dramatist Ji Junxiang.

Manning went to Cambridge University one year after the French Revolution. Both the French and earlier American revolutions were important events to the Romantics. By 1802 he was in Paris seeking a Chinese teacher and wrote home that he found the revolutionary/republican atmosphere inspiring and had dined with Tom Paine and the linguist William Taylor. More importantly for his quest to learn Chinese he made acquaintance with Joseph Hager, the Keeper of Oriental Manuscripts at the Bibliothèque Nationale, as Weech says, 'his first opportunity to learn from a self-professed authority on China'.

After meeting Hager, Manning's desire to get to China was accelerated. He wrote to his father, back in his hometown of Diss, 'I shall never be happy till I am settled, but I have many things to do first. I certainly mean if possible to penetrate the interior of China.' And in another letter, his forming of a specialist interest within China studies, 'Chinese manners are a subject that much interests me.'

However, circumstances intervened. War between Britain and France in the first Napoleonic Wars meant Manning's China ambitions were temporarily thwarted. Still in Paris he was arrested and imprisoned as a *prisonnier de guerre* in 1804. Once back in England he focused on China and sought patronage. He approached such luminaries as Joseph Banks at the Royal Society and anybody else who could put in a good word for him with the EIC—still the gatekeepers for those seeking passage to China. Despite acquiring additional materials and meeting several Chinese in Paris Manning's language skills were still rudimentary at best, but he hoped that if the EIC could get him to Canton he could seriously work on them.

Eventually the EIC offered Manning passage to Canton and a room in the Factories. They warned him though that hazards abounded—the journey would be long, round the horn to China in this pre-Suez period, and EIC ships were threatened by raids from the French Navy. Once in Canton the mortality rate for foreigners was alarmingly high.

He was also at the whim of the EIC's commercial decision. In Manning's case this meant an enforced six-month sojourn enroute to China in Penang. However, here, at last, Manning could have his first semi-coherent conversation with a 'real' Chinese person. He spent his time in Georgetown improving his Chinese and had finally arrived off the coast of China and was heading towards Canton in January 1807. Momentarily fears of French raiders gave way to fears of Chinese pirates but they made the Pearl River and Canton.

Manning lived in the Factories, essentially the warehouses, mess halls and dormitories for the foreigners in the China Trade. But they were confined to the small area, cut off largely from the 'real China', technically forbidden to leave, though small illicit excursions into the city were occasionally made to relieve the tedium of life inside the Factories. The only other option was that when the trading finished everyone returned to sojourn for six months at Macao.

Weech writes that Manning started dressing like a Chinese after he arrived in Canton. A slight frustration was that he desperately wanted to perfect his Mandarin but only ever heard Cantonese in and around the Factories. There was a slight siege mentality among the British in Canton and Macao too—the Royal Navy heightened its presence in the South China Seas during the Napoleonic Wars to protect Britain's China Trade from French interference.

Weech details Manning's multivarious attempts to penetrate interior China. He was denied entry via Cochinchina over the border and ended up in the Paracel Islands, totally uninteresting to Manning, instead. The trip was a total waste of time. He wanted to smuggle himself into China up the coast as a number of missionaries had, but the EIC forbade it. Ultimately China's long land borders were the answer and a side trip to Calcutta in 1810 enabled a border crossing via Bhutan and into Tibet. Manning aimed to head for Lhasa and then onwards to Peking, Nanjing and finally back to Canton overland—a quite epic journey.

Manning knew only a minuscule amount about Tibet. In 1810 the western archive on that country was tiny. He later wrote that in Tibet, 'the Chinese lord it like the English in India'. But, as mentioned above, he was suspected of being a missionary or a spy and sent back to India.

Peking was forbidden to all but a handful of Europeans in the early 1800s. However, the announcement of the Amherst Embassy in 1816 reignited hopes of penetrating the interior at long last. Manning signed on as a translator to the Mission. Time with a teacher in Canton as well as his Tibet misadventure seems to have ensured that his Chinese improved significantly, though the more straight-laced Amherst was apparently aghast at Manning's penchant for a big unruly beard and his Chinese gowns. Of course, the kowtow controversy scuppered the Mission which stayed less than a day in Peking. To Manning, it was a devastating blow and a brief glimpse of his long yearned for objective. He did get to nose around a few spots—in Anhui—but even there the local booksellers were forbidden to sell him texts.

By the time he arrived back in Canton in 1817 Manning had been away a decade. He decided to return home, but adventure followed him. He was shipwrecked off Java but managed to survive and board another ship which was calling at St Helena, by then Napoleon's prison. This was the first indication that anyone outside his small circle in the Factories and the EIC had been paying any attention to his life. Apparently Napoleon requested to meet Manning, this Englishman who had met the Grand Lama of Tibet no less.

Ever the polymath, once he got back to England Manning wrote a treatise on tea in Tibet. He continued his study of Chinese, and especially wrote about the Chinese sense of humour—an interesting insight on Chinese society and power structures. As he had written to his father when embarking on his decade long trip East, he wanted to study Chinese manners.

He remained true to his Romantic roots too. Manning's aim was to humanise the little known and lesser understood Chinese to a British audience. To set them to interrogate their pervasive notions of cultural superiority more critically. By now he reputedly had the finest Chinese library in Europe. He was a Sinologist, consulted by those newly enthralled by the study and promise of China, a recognised expert in the field.

Thomas Manning died in 1840 in relative obscurity. He left behind fragments—Tibetan tea, language notes, his essays on the Chinese sense of humour—but no truly great body of work. And, ultimately, he was unable to influence British public opinion prior to the First Opium War (1839-1842) that raged as he died. As Weech says finally,

'Even so, history did not end there. And Manning's forward-thinking project may yet have more resonance in our day than it did in his own'.

Edward Weech has successfully rescued one of Britain's earliest Sinologues from obscurity and for that he should be thanked. That he has written such a highly readable and engaging biography of the man is really the cream on the coffee that makes *Chinese Dreams in Romantic England* an important study of early Sinology.

Paul French *is the author of* Midnight in Peking, *a New York Times Bestseller, and* City of Devils: A Shanghai Noir. *His next book* Her Lotus Year: The Mysterious China Sojourn of the Woman Who Became the Duchess of Windsor *will be published in 2024.*

AUTOBIOGRAPHY OF A CHINESE WOMAN

By Buwei Yang Chao

Camphor Press, 2020

Reviewed by Jen Lin-Liu

Towards the end of *Autobiography of a Chinese Woman*, author Buwei Yang Chao writes about a visit to Washington D.C. in the mid 1940s with her four daughters and her husband. After scrutinizing Abraham Lincoln's face for a hint of a smile at his memorial on the mall and visiting the Tomb of the Unknown Soldier, the family wraps up their outing.

> "Let's go home", one of us said, meaning our hotel in Washington.
> "Let's go home", said another, thinking of Walker Street and the fall term.
> "Yes, let's go home", said still another, dreaming of Lanchia Chuang and Yenliang Hsiang.

Without specifically mentioning who says what, the attuned reader knows that it is the author's husband Yuenren Chao who considers Walker Street in Cambridge, Massachusetts 'home' while Buwei Yang Chao is dreaming of China.

When Buwei Yang Chao's *Autobiography of a Chinese Woman* was published in 1947, it garnered good reviews from publications like *The New York Times* but was a commercial flop. Its publication came two years after Richard Walsh, the founder of publishers John Day Company and husband of Pearl S. Buck, released Chao's groundbreaking cookbook *How to Cook and Eat in Chinese*. Chao's cookbook was a runaway success. It sold hundreds of thousands of copies over three decades and twenty-two printings. It is regrettable that Chao's memoir was not more successful for, even as a food writer, I found the memoir even more charming and insightful than her landmark cookbook. And fortunately for readers, *Autobiography of a Chinese Woman* has been republished digitally by Taiwan's Camphor Classics in the last decade. (Book buyers be aware: Amazon currently sells a pirated edition of the book under a dubious publisher called

Chosho—the Chao family is currently investigating how to remove this from the site's listings.) Readers who have lived in both China and the West, felt the pull of two different worlds, and are interested in the lives of notable figures from the Republican era will be most rewarded by the read.

The person who features most prominently is the author's husband Yuenren Chao, a linguist who is considered one of Tsinghua University's 'Four Big' Masters and is famous in China and Chinese diaspora communities for his 1930s hit song *How Can I Help Thinking of Her*. In fact, Yuenren narrates the book's foreword, which begins with how the book came into being and how his wife only began writing it recently. But then, in vaudeville-like style, Chao herself cuts in with 'No, Yuenren, you are all mixed up…' Her husband once again begins to narrate before Chao cuts in again, and then takes over completely, giving readers a good sense of the dominating personality that Chao could be. A story that members of the Chao family like to tell is of when the noted historian John Fairbank and his wife Wilma once came over to the Chao house. Chao found Wilma so haughty that she gave her a verbal lashing that had her leaving the house in tears.

After Chao confidently takes over as the narrator, she gives readers an introduction to how she is 'a typical Chinese woman'. She has 'much power in the family', but she lets her 'husband decide on the important things, which are few and far between'. 'I compare my daughters' pretty looks with mine at their age with satisfaction; I compare my parties with those of Mrs. Chao Three and Mrs. Lee Four', she writes. She notes she has the 'voice of a second alto. When I say "Hello" over the telephone and the other party says, "May I speak to Mrs. Chao?" I say, "This *is* Mrs. Chao"'.

The short, fifty chapters that follow narrate her upbringing in a multigenerational, noble family in Nanjing in the 1890s; the unique education that her grandfather encouraged her to receive that made her one of China's first female physicians, and her marriage and family life abroad in the United States with Yuenren Chao.

Chao's writing style was heavily influenced by her friend Hu Shih, the founder of a literary movement in China that compelled authors to write in the vernacular, and who happened to be one of two guests invited to the simple wedding she and Yuenren held in 1921. Her writing style is clear and direct, and exemplified by the fact that she liked 'open issues openly discussed'. Other historic characters who make an appearance in the memoir include the Chinese war hero Zeng Guofan, who employed Chao's grandfather Yang Renshan, himself a notable Buddhist scholar and government official, British scholar Timothy Richard, philosopher Bertrand Russell, Russell's second wife, Dora Black Russell, and author Pearl S. Buck who once chastised Chao by saying that 'Chinese residents in America did not mix enough with Americans'.

Yuenren's career took them to the United States, where he taught at universities including Harvard and Yale and was an administrator for the Chinese Educational Mission in Washington D.C. The couple, and their growing family in the 1920s and 1930s, split their time between China and the United States. They settled in Nanjing in the 1930s, just before the Japanese invasion and the Rape of Nanjing, and ended up fleeing to Changsha and Kunming, where academics at Tsinghua, Nankai, and Peking University united, during the war, to create the National Southwestern Associated University.

The book ends shortly after Chao's cookbook is published and after the couple's children have graduated from high school and are attending college. Three of their four daughters graduated from Radcliffe College, and each went on to illustrious careers in musicology, chemistry, writing, and astrophysics. The book ends with a cliffhanger—the Chaos decide to move back to China and it is the late 1940s, just before the Communist Revolution.

It turned out that en route to China, the Chaos stopped at the University of California Berkeley, where Yuenren was offered a professorship. He took the position, not because they were aware of the impending Communist takeover, but because Chao convinced Yuenren that he would not enjoy being a university president, the job that awaited him in China.

The lack of narrative structure is the main weakness of the book. Despite the fascinating life she led, the chapters begin to feel a bit plodding and aimless, as is the case with many memoirs. And Chao, strangely, glossed over or completely neglected to mention certain challenges she faced, including foot binding imposed by her female guardians in her childhood, racism in the United States, and the trauma of Japan's invasion of China. These moments will be amplified in a biography that I am currently writing about Chao, tentatively titled *The Formidable Mrs. Chao*.

Jen Lin-Liu (jen@jenlinliu.com) is the author of Serve the People: A Stir-Fried Journey through China, On the Noodle Road: From Beijing to Rome with Love and Pasta, *and the forthcoming* The Formidable Mrs. Chao. *She is the events director and a culinary consultant for Chang Chang, a restaurant in Washington D.C. by Peter Chang. You can contact her on Instagram @jenlinliu or at jen@jenlinliu.com.*

CHEN JIANLIN—A LIFE DEDICATED TO HISTORY

BY KATHERINE SONG

Chinese Director Chen Jialin 陈家林 was a prominent name in Chinese film-making, famed for his films and television series on historical subjects. In his lifetime he produced more than thirty historical dramas, among which *Kangxi Dynasty*, *Wu Ze Tian* and *Kingdom of Heavenly Peace* signify his highest achievements. Unlike many fifth and sixth generation film directors whose

Figure 1: Chen Jialin

works travelled internationally, Chen's dramas were predominantly made for China. They covered a wide span of history and depicted emperors of the Qin, Han, Tang, Ming, and Qing dynasties, as well as disputable religious and folklore figures. His television shows were often the 'talk of the town'. He died on 7 July 2022 at age 79.

Chen was born in Nanjing in 1943. At the age of twelve he starred in the film *Luo Xiaotolin's Determination*, playing the protagonist Luo Xiaolin. He later studied acting at the Beijing Film Academy and in 1965 was assigned to the Changchun Film Studio in Jilin Province as an actor. Nothing is recorded about his acting career in the following decade, but in 1978 he re-emerged as a director. His first film *Birds on an Island* was an environmental documentary which immediately won him an award from China's Ministry of Culture. In 1984 he debuted his first history film *Tan Sitong* 谭嗣同, a screen adaptation of a die-hard reformer who was executed by the Qing government following the failure of the Hundred Day Reforms in 1898. The picture won him the second Best Film prize, as rated by the Ministry of Culture.

When television sets became ubiquitous in China's households, Chen directed his first television series *Nurhachi* 努尔哈赤 (1986), a biographical drama of the Jurchen leader who united all the northern tribes in the late 16th century and is deemed the founding father of the later Qing Dynasty. The series won the First Prize in China's Television Feitian (Flying in Sky) Awards. Chen himself received the laurel of

Best Director.

For the ensuing three decades Chen was prolific in film and television production, especially in television series. All were broadcast at prime time on China's Central Television (CCTV) and widely watched. Many were highly regarded and became extremely popular. He also began to cast film stars in some of the major roles. His film *The Last Empress* 最后的皇后 (1987) starring Pan Hong 潘虹 and Jiang Wen 姜文 won the Special Jury Award at the 4th Brasilia International Film and Television Festival. *Baise Uprising* 白色起义 (1990), a story about Deng Xiaoping's 邓小平 early career won him the Excellent Film Award of the Ministry of Media. *Emperor Tang Ming* 唐明皇 (1992) won the 11th Golden Eagle Award for a long series and special achievement recognition at the 13th Feitian Awards. His filmography and television series of history dramas also include:

Empress Yang 杨贵妃 (1992) starring Zhou Jie 周洁

Wu Ze Tian 武则天 (1993) starring Liu Xiaoqing 刘晓庆

Snows on Helan Mountains 贺兰雪 (1995) starring Wu Gang 巫刚 and Li Jianqun 李建群

Flying Swallows in the Han Palace 汉宫双燕 (1996) starring Zhang Tielin 张铁林 and Zhao Mingming 赵明明

Emperor Han Wu 汉武帝 (1996) starring Zhou Lijing 周里京

Taiping Heavenly Kingdom 太平天国 (1998) starring Gao Lancun 高蓝村

Kangxi Dynasty 康熙王朝, (2001) co-directed with Liu Dayin 刘大印, starring Chen Daoming 陈道明 and Siqin Gaowa 斯琴高娃

Diao Chan 貂蝉 (2002) starring Sharia Zhang 张敏 and Lv Liangwei 吕良伟

The Affair in the Swing Age 江山风雨情 (2003) starring Li Qing 李强 and Liu Wei 刘威

A Hundred Years of the Sea 沧海百年 (2004) starring Gui Yalei 归亚蕾 and Zhu Xu 朱旭

The Great Qing Dynasty 大清帝国 (2005) starring Jiang Wen 姜文 and Zhang Fengyi 张丰毅

Wang Zhaojun 王昭君 (2005) starring Yang Mi 杨幂

The Great Dunhuang 大敦煌 (2006) starring Tang Guoqiang 唐国强

War Between Chu and Han 楚汉之争 (2011) starring Huang Qiusheng 黄秋生

In addition, Chen co-directed *Land War of Jiawu*甲午陆战, *Liao Zhai—Strange Tales from a Make-do Studio* 聊斋, *Expressway of Great Qin* 大秦直道 and *A Hundred Year of Flowing Clouds* 百年虚云. In 2010's version of *Romance of the Three Kingdoms* 三国, Chen was honoured by being appointed as Chief Advisor to the production.

Chen's dramas are characterised by riveting plots, complex and conflicting personalities and tortuous flows of events. Crowd pleasing as they were, none was deemed frivolous. Asked what made his series successful, Chen summarised:

> [...] the history drama is more than literary and artistic work. I have three principles for screen creation. First the large historical background and context must be accurate, and the important events must have really existed. Before I embark [on] a new project, I solicit the opinions of historians. The main characters depicted on screen are generally conformed to the historical evaluation of them. The rest is set according to the need of the plot.

This made Chen a screen master; mixing history, art and literature in an effortless perfection that could easily stir the feelings of his audience. In his limelight Chinese dynasties are filled with court intrigues, internecine feuds, concubine in-fights, and ruthless competition for power. Emperors are revered and feared but also victims of their own imbecility. In front of their subjects they hold heavenly mandates but back in their private quarters they are tormented by loneliness, betrayal, self-doubt, family schisms and threats on all fronts. In *Kangxi Dynasty*, Chen covered the emperor's lifespan of more than 60 years, from his ascent to the throne at age five until his death at sixty-eight, a long and turbulent reign tested incessantly by war, rebellion and conspiracies of all sorts. In his precocious youth Kangxi is ambitious but taught to be resilient and tenacious. In the heyday of his career he is valorous, just and victorious, defeats his enemies one by one and establishes the vast Qing Empire. Chen's scenes describing an emperor's old age are often the most memorable and illuminating. There is an astonishing degree of similarity among all his emperors once they get old. At senility, ambition and sanity go, along with the loss of physical vigour. The emperors become indolent, suspicious and cruel, often making wrong decisions about their most loyal and devoted officials and their family members, who find demotion, imprisonment and even ordered-suicide (賜死) as their bitter ends. Such depictions could easily strike a chord with the Chinese audience, who may have experienced similar episodes of history.

Painful and dark can history be, what is steadfast and consistent in all Chen's works is a central theme of unity, a welcoming position for his market. For instance in *Kangxi Dynasty* (2001) Chen goes to great lengths in describing the threats facing the emperor's reign and his resolve in asserting territorial integrity at all costs. In Chen's assessment, Kangxi's victory over Wu Sangui's 吳三桂 rebellion, his defeat of Zheng Jing 郑经 in Taiwan and his crushing of Galdan's 葛尔丹 military aggression in the north are Kangxi's defining achievements and what makes him, unequivocally, a great emperor. His cunning and shrewdness, selfishness and mistakes made to his kith and kin were secondary and should deserve to be forgiven and even forgotten. Chen's dramas are not history books, however they render historical insights and intellectual depth that could compel his audience to ponder. That might simply be Chen's altruistic purpose; he wants the audience to think and reflect when watching his dramas.

Director Chen was never married. He once commented that his works were his off-spring. His life-partner Li Jianqun 李建群 was an accomplished costume designer who crafted thousands of beautiful outfits for Chen's shows. She also often played a role in Chen's series. The most memorable was Empress Rong 容妃 in *Kangxi Dynasty*, the emperor's loving concubine who eventually fell out of favour, was abandoned and tragically died in a 'cold palace'(冷宫). Li Jianqun died in 2020 at the age of 63.

On 8 July 2022 the Directing Committee of China's Broadcasting Federation announced Chen's death and published a eulogy recognizing Chen's stellar career. The homage paid by such a government agency asserts Chen's preeminent status in the directing sphere. It acclaims that:

> The death of Director Chen Jialin is a huge loss to China's television drama industry. He was a well-respected leading figure and his works helped elevate the overall equality of screen creation. His tremendous contribution to standardizing and regulating the TV market as well as his advocacy for rights of the directing profession

were unforgettable. His advice was invaluable and his pragmatism yielded positive changes. We mourn him with deep sorrows. May he rest in peace.

Katherine Song *(kyqsong@hotmail.com) is a management consultant specialising in project management and leadership development. Born and raised in Beijing, she has lived and worked in Hong Kong, Canada and the United States of America before moving to Shanghai in 2006. She serves as a Council Member of the Royal Asiatic Society China and has convened its Film Club since 2019.*

IN MEMORY OF ISABEL CROOK 1915-2023

by Melinda Liu and Tracey Willard

Born in Sichuan Province, Isabel
Crook was the daughter of Canadian
missionaries, an anthropologist, an
educator and a 'participant-observer
in the Chinese Communist revolution',
as she put it. She witnessed the demise
of the Qing Dynasty, two world wars,
China's warlord period and Republican
era, and the victory of the Chinese
communist regime.

After a childhood in Chengdu,
Isabel went to Canada for study, and
returned in 1939, intent on conducting

Figure 1: Isabel Crook.

anthropological research among Yi minority communities. She met
her husband David in Chengdu in the early 1940s; he had come to
China as a ComIntern agent, though later became disillusioned with
his handlers. They moved to London, married there in 1942, then
returned to China. Together they studied land reform and observed
life in rural areas, until entering Beijing in 1949 alongside communist
supporters who had won China's civil war. They were invited by
Chinese Communist Party leaders to help set up a new foreign
languages school in Beijing which became the Beijing Foreign Studies
University. There they helped train several generations of Chinese
diplomats over four decades.

In 1981 Isabel retired from teaching, turning once again to
anthropological research. The work that she had done in partnership
with other anthropologists, and her field notes from the 1940's,
eventually led to the 2013 publication of *Prosperity's Predicament;
Identity, Reform, and Resistance in Rural Wartime China*. The book was
launched at an event in Beijing at The Bookworm, introduced by the
RASBJ. In 2019 she was awarded the China Friendship Medal by Xi
Jinping in person.

A friend who knew the couple described Isabel as 'nice, but
frankly, so much character scares the hell out of me!' according to her

Financial Times obituary. She had lived most of her life in China, and died in Beijing at the age of 107. Isabel is survived by her three sons, six grandchildren and nine great-grandchildren.

Figure 2: A male friend described Isabel as 'nice, but frankly, so much character scares the hell out of me'.

Printed in the USA
CPSIA information can be obtained
at www.ICGtesting.com
LVHW050903210424
777879LV00019B/440